Maud Gonne

Maud Gonne

TRISH FERGUSON

Published on behalf of
the Historical Association of Ireland
by

UNIVERSITY COLLEGE DUBLIN PRESS
Preas Choláiste Ollscoile Bhaile Átha Cliath
2019

First published 2019 on behalf of the
Historical Association of Ireland by
University College Dublin Press

© Trish Ferguson, 2019

ISBN 978-1-910820-24-7
ISSN 2009-1397

University College Dublin Press
UCD Humanities Institute
Dublin 4, Ireland
www.ucdpress.ie

Cataloguing in Publication data available from the British Library

Typeset in Scotland in Ehrhardt by Ryan Shiels
Text design by Lyn Davies
Printed in Dublin on acid-free paper by
SPRINT-print

CONTENTS

Foreword   *vii*

Acknowledgements   *ix*

Chronology of Gonne's Life and Times   *xi*

   Introduction   *I*

1 The Early Years: A Republican Education   *7*

2 Dublin and Donegal   *14*

3 The New Speranza   *24*

4 Ireland's Joan of Arc   *36*

5 Inghinidhe na hÉireann   *42*

6 Maud Gonne MacBride   *59*

7 The Rising and After   *71*

8 The Treaty and After   *79*

   Conclusion   *88*

Notes   *92*

Select Biographical Details   *113*

Index   *121*

FOREWORD

Originally conceived over a decade ago to place the lives of leading figures in Irish history against the background of new research on the problems and conditions of their times and modern assessments of their historical significance, the Historical Association of Ireland Life and Times series enjoyed remarkable popularity and success. A second series has now been planned in association with UCD Press in a new format and with fuller scholarly apparatus. Encouraged by the reception given to the earlier series, the volumes in the new series will be expressly designed to be of particular help to students preparing for the Leaving Certificate, for GCE Advanced Level and for undergraduate history courses, as well as appealing to the happily insatiable appetite for new views of Irish history among the general public.

CIARAN BRADY
Historical Association of Ireland

To Cliodna McAleer

*

ACKNOWLEDGEMENTS

I would like to extend warm thanks to Ciaran Brady for inviting me to contribute to the Historical Association of Ireland's Life and Times New Series and for helpful advice throughout the process of writing this volume. Thanks also are due to Ruth Hallinan and Conor Graham at UCD Press for prompt and valuable guidance.

I am deeply indebted to the British Academy for the grant that enabled me to carry out archival work on Maud Gonne at Emory University and also to the Stuart A. Rose Manuscript, Archives and Rare Book Library for granting me a fellowship to support this research. Particular thanks are extended to Kathleen Shoemaker at the Rose Library for her help with accessing materials in the archives during my stay at Emory University and for providing the cover image of Gonne for this volume.

I also have a number of groups and individuals to thank for feedback on my research and on drafts of this volume. Particular thanks are due to Elizabeth Mannion and Sonja Tiernan for their generous, helpful and incisive feedback on drafts. I am also very grateful to Donna Mitchell for inviting me to speak on Gonne at Mary Immaculate College's 1916 commemorative programme in Limerick and to the members of staff and students who attended and gave helpful direction in discussions. Also, thanks to Terry Phillips and my colleagues in the Irish Studies Research Group at Liverpool Hope University for feedback on papers delivered on Gonne over the course of my research.

Thanks, as always, are offered with love to my family, particularly my father, Sean Ferguson, for translating some of Gonne's letters, and to Colin, for being brilliant, always. I also extend heartfelt thanks to a number of friends who provided much in the way of encouragement, support and, at times, welcome distractions over the course of this project, notably William Blazek, Jane Carroll, Darryl Jones, Brian McAleer, Una McAleer, Dee McKiernan, Elizabeth Mannion, Donna Mitchell, Erica Mitchell and all belonging to 64, but most of all to Cliodna McAleer, to whom this book is dedicated.

TRISH FERGUSON
March 2019

CHRONOLOGY OF GONNE'S LIFE
AND TIMES

1866

Edith Maud Gonne is born on 21 December in Tongham, Surrey.

1868

In April the Gonne family relocate to Ireland when Tommy Gonne is stationed in the Curragh, County Kildare. Maud's sister, Kathleen, is born in September.

1871

Margaretta Gonne is born in June. Edith Gonne, Maud's mother, dies shortly after childbirth and Margaretta dies on 9 August. Tommy secures a house in Donnybrook for Maud and Kathleen who are placed under the care of a governess.

1876

Gonne's father is appointed military attaché to the Austrian court. Maud and Kathleen are sent to live in London with their aunt Augusta.

1885

Colonel Gonne is appointed Assistant Adjutant-General for Dublin. Maud and Kathleen return to live in Dublin.

1886

Gonne's father dies on 30 November. Maud and Kathleen relocate to London to live with their uncle William.

1887

Gonne visits Royat to recover from illness in the summer. Here she meets Lucien Millevoye, a right-wing journalist who is working with Boulangist associates. They form a republican alliance, vowing to work together to restore Alsace-Lorraine to France and overturn British rule in Ireland. Turning 21 in December, Gonne attains her inheritance and relocates to Dublin.

1889

Gonne meets W. B. Yeats for the first time on 30 January. She immerses herself in Irish culture during this year, attending meetings of the Contemporary Society on Nassau Street, Dublin and embarks on a course of reading in Irish history in the National Library.

1890

Gonne gives birth to a son, Georges, on 11 January (fathered by Millevoye). She works with evicted tenants in Donegal in the spring and makes a political speech in Barrow-in-Furness for a Liberal candidate in a by-election.

1891

Georges dies on 31 August. Gonne takes comfort in Yeats's friendship and joins the Order of the Golden Dawn as she explores the possibility of reincarnation.

1892

Gonne tours France, Holland and Belgium in the summer, publicising the draconian treatment of Irish tenants in the course of the evictions. She publishes her first article 'Un Peuple Opprimé' in *La Revue International* and writes a series, 'Le Martyre de L'Irlande' for *Journal des Voyages*.

1893

Gonne visits prisoners in Portland Jail.

1894

Gonne gives birth to a daughter, Iseult, on 6 August, having had inter-
course with Millevoye the previous year at the crypt where Georges
was buried in the hope that his spirit could be reincarnated.

1897

Gonne establishes an Irish nationalist newspaper, *L'Irlande Libre*, in Paris.
Gonne and Yeats found L'Association Irlandaise, the Paris Branch of
the Young Ireland League. With James Connolly, Gonne helps to
organise a demonstration in opposition to Queen Victoria's Diamond
Jubilee celebrations in Dublin. This involves a symbolic mock-funeral
for the British Empire, represented by a coffin that was thrown into the
River Liffey. Gonne tours America from October to December, lectur-
ing on Ireland under British rule, to raise money for the centenary
celebrations of the 1898 rebellion led by Wolfe Tone.

1898

Gonne oversees the production of articles for *L'Irlande Libre* to commem-
orate the 1898 centenary. In February she visits Belmullet, County Mayo,
which is in the midst of famine. She rallies tenants to resist conditions
imposed with work offered on the roads and convinces the Belmullet
Board of Guardians to meet demands for higher pay. With James
Connolly she writes a pamphlet 'The right to life and the rights of
property', which justifies stealing on the plea of necessity. She travels to
Sligo, Dublin, Paris and London, during which time she communicates
regularly with Yeats on their dreams, which culminates in a 'spiritual
marriage' in December.

1899

Gonne attends eviction meetings in Mayo in May, and then returns to
Dublin to advocate for political prisoners. In October she establishes a
Transvaal Committee in response to news of the Boer War which broke
out in September. She is a central figure in a public protest against the

presentation of an honorary degree to the Colonial Secretary, Joseph Chamberlain, by charging through Beresford Place in a brake with a Transvaal flag.

1900

Gonne embarks on a second lecture tour of America from January to March. In April, she founds Inghinidhe na hÉireann (Daughters of Ireland). She writes an article entitled 'The Famine Queen' in response to the visit of Queen Victoria which was in aid of recruitment of Irish soldiers for the British war against the Boers. She also organises a 'Patriotic Children's Treat' in Clonturk Park in response to a similar event hosted in the name of Queen Victoria during her visit to Dublin. She meets John MacBride in Paris.

1901

Gonne embarks on a lecture tour of America with John MacBride.

1902

Gonne agrees to marry John MacBride. She also plays the role of Cathleen ni Houlihan to a packed theatre in Clarendon Street Hall, Dublin.

1903

Gonne converts to Catholicism in February and marries MacBride in Paris on 21 February. Gonne stages a public protest in the Rotunda at a meeting regarding the visit of King Edward VII. She also stages a protest at her home in Coulson Avenue, raising a black flag which, she says, is in mourning for the Pope. The demonstration escalates into a 'siege' that is reported in the newspapers.

1904

Gonne gives birth to a son, Seán MacBride, on 26 January. She writes the play *Dawn*, which is published in *United Irishman*. In May she tells Yeats that she has made a disastrous error in her marriage. In December she seeks legal advice on getting a divorce.

1905

Gonne files for separation from John MacBride. On 8 August 1906 a Paris court rules in favour of the separation with Gonne and she is granted custody of Seán. She decides to remain resident in France with Iseult and Seán.

1908

Gonne is involved in establishing the feminist nationalist paper *Bean na hÉireann*, edited by Helena Molony.

1911

Gonne initiates a school meals programme in Dublin based on the Canticus Scolaires model that had been adopted successfully in France.

1913

For much of the year Gonne organises food for poor children in Dublin and for the families of striking workers in the 1913 Lockout.

1914

With Iseult, Gonne serves as a nurse in French military hospitals.

1916

Upon hearing of the 1916 Rising and the plans to execute its leaders, including her husband, Gonne tries urgently to return to Dublin but is barred from travelling by the British War Office. She appeals to Yeats to help her secure a passport.

1917

Arriving in Southampton in September 1917 Gonne is served with the Defence of the Realm Act, disbarring her from travelling to Ireland. She stays in London with Eva Gore-Booth and manages to escape surveillance by leaving Turkish baths in disguise, which allows her to return to Dublin.

1918

Lord French releases a proclamation on 18 May 1918 alleging a conspiracy between Sinn Féin and the German Empire to start an armed insurrection in Ireland. Gonne is taken into custody for printing literature deemed to be seditious and is sent to England where she is interned in Holloway.

1921

Peace negotiations in London result in the Treaty which creates an Irish Free State within the British Empire for 26 counties of Ireland. Civil war breaks out. Gonne forms The Women's Peace Committee to try to reconcile the Free State and republican sides.

1922

Gonne and Charlotte Despard form the Women's Prisoners' Defence League which establishes the Irish Republican Prisoners' Dependents' Fund. Working for Desmond Fitzgerald, Minister of Publicity, Gonne goes to Paris to publicise the conditions in which Catholics are living in Belfast at the hands of Orangemen and Freemasons.

1923

Gonne is arrested in April under Cosgrave's Coercion Act of 1923 due to her demonstrations with the Women's Prisoners' Defence League. She is released after 20 days during which time she was on hunger strike.

1931

Gonne is made Chair of the National Aid Association, formed to support republicans forced out of employment.

1937

The Irish State ratifies the Constitution. Gonne establishes *Prison Bars*, a monthly newssheet of the Women's Prisoners' Defence League founded to publicise the treatment of political prisoners. She rejects the terms of de Valera's constitution through the pages of *Prison Bars*.

1938

Gonne's memoir, *A Servant of the Queen*, is published.

1939

Yeats dies in France. Gonne writes a chapter on 'Yeats and Ireland' for a collection of essays written in tribute.

1949

The Republic of Ireland Act comes into force in April. In an interview for Radio Éireann, Gonne emphasises the achievements of Inghinidhe na hÉireann.

1953

Gonne dies of cardiac failure at Roebuck House, Clonskeagh on 27 April. She is buried in Glasnevin Cemetery.

Introduction

In 1937, as the people of the Irish State ratified the current Irish Constitution, Maud Gonne committed to posterity her account of her contribution to the birth of a Republic. The ironic title of her memoir, *A Servant of the Queen*, echoes the battle between Queen Maeve, the mythical warrior Queen of Ireland against the 'Famine Queen', Victoria, under whose despotic rule millions had died from starvation or were forced to emigrate.

Within this account of activism in the service of Ireland, Gonne gleefully tells a tale of a battle of wills between her and a neighbouring English family at a time when she was residing in France for health reasons and also, she claimed, under threat of imprisonment if she returned to Ireland.[1] From the balcony of her rented apartment, she hung an Irish flag to celebrate St Patrick's Day. Her neighbours reported her flag to the police, who asked Gonne to take it down as it was illegal to fly any flag other than the French flag, and even this was only allowed on 14 July. They also complained that Gonne kept late hours with visitors staying until the early morning. Failing to resolve the issue through their landlord, her neighbours bought a hunting horn and started making noise first thing in the morning. However, as this was against French law, at Gonne's request the police made them stop. The daughter of the family then started playing the violin at 7 a.m. each morning. Gonne retaliated by staying up when the family had gone

to bed, lifting a log from the fireplace and dropping it inter-
mittently on the floor. When the landlord complained on behalf of
the English family, Gonne acquired a note from a doctor she knew
that read that 'Mademoiselle Gonne suffered from a nervous complaint and that whenever her sleep in the morning was disturbed in
any way by any musical instrument, the nervous complaint caused
her such shakiness of hand that she was apt to drop anything she
held, especially toward the evening, when she tired.'[2] When the
English family gave notice to quit the apartment, Gonne gave their
address to hundreds of her student friends telling them that the
family residing there were leaving, and that they had a hunting
horn and a violin for sale. This anecdote, which Gonne recounts
with relish, is beautifully characteristic, serving well to illustrate
how she loved to take tactics used against her, however trivial, and
deploy them herself against her antagonist in a counter war.

Gonne's temperament made her eminently suited to engage in
a propaganda battle with England. She laid out the scope of this
battle in military terms: 'Lines of communication,' she asserted,
'must be established between Ireland's children in America and
Ireland's children at home; between France, the leader of the Celtic
countries, and Ireland, the ancient Centre of the Celtic race.'[3] Gonne
took up the pen as her 'only available weapon' early in her political
life, when, following the advice of her lover, Lucien Millevoye, she
left the practical work of helping evicted tenants in Ireland and
turned her efforts instead toward publicising – in French and
American publications – the condition of Ireland under British
rule.[4] In *The American Irish and their Influence on Irish Politics*
(1882), Philip H. Bagenal argued that hostility expressed toward
Ireland in descriptions of the Irish as demons, vermin and scum by
the London press rankled deeper than Coercion Acts and the
treatment of Irish prisoners.[5] Given that the American press took

their information on Irish affairs from English news agencies, Gonne sought to directly engage with the American press, embarking on three lecture tours of America in 1897, 1900 and 1901. In 1901, Gonne complained:

> It is impossible for Irish Americans to know what is passing in Ireland. England controls the cables; England controls the news-agencies, and the American press takes its news from news-agencies or from correspondents living in London, who in their turn take their information of Irish affairs from English news-agencies. I have read American accounts of events in Ireland so distorted that none would recognise them, and the distortion is always to the disadvantage of the nationalists.[6]

With her striking looks, wealth and numerous contacts, Gonne was well placed to give her first-hand account of Ireland under British rule through the international press. Maire Comerford believed that 'there may not have been another person in all Ireland with the contacts she had abroad' and that there was 'no paper wall she could not break through.'[7] As well as becoming one of the most prolific Irish nationalist writers of the early twentieth century, Gonne was able to personally finance Arthur Griffith and Willie Rooney's nationalist paper, *United Irishman*. She also went on to found and distribute *Bean na hÉireann*, a newspaper for nationalist Irishwomen and *Prison Bars*, the organ of the Womens' Prisoners Defence League, which highlighted the living conditions suffered by political prisoners and campaigned for their release. In her final interview in 1953, as she looked back on her life, she noted that by the time a Liberal government in England pledged to end evictions and to bring in a Home Rule bill, she had 'made a big breach in the Wall of Silence.'[8]

While many studies of Gonne's life have critiqued the self-aggrandisement of her autobiography, it was a much-needed reclamation of the narrative of Irish independence for revolutionary women who for many years were neglected in favour of the romanticised glorification of the 16 men who lost their lives in the British retribution for the Easter Rising. Recent years have witnessed a much more comprehensive view of the events of 1916, with commemorations examining the significance of the lives of figures often marginalised in studies of the political arena, notably women who were barred from joining nationalist organisations. In 2016, a collaborative project entitled 'Women of the Rising' celebrated Kathleen Lynn, Constance Markievicz, Helena Molony, Elizabeth O'Farrell, Mary Perolz and Margaret Skinnider and yet the iconic and celebrated figure of Maud Gonne was omitted, so that she remains, for many, primarily remembered as the beloved muse of Yeats.

Her legendary beauty and her connection with Yeats and MacBride, which served her political purposes, has led to a reductive approach to biographical studies of her life. Samuel Levenson's *Maud Gonne: A Biography of Yeats's Beloved* (1977) and, more recently, Kathryn Kirkpatrick's *Her Small Hands Were Not Beautiful* (2018) and Adrian Frazier's *The Adulterous Muse: Maud Gonne, Lucien Millevoye and W. B. Yeats* (2016) focus on the romantic life of Gonne. Likewise, Barry Shortall's *Willie and Maud: A Love Story* (2002) and Margery Brady's *Love Story of Yeats and Maud Gonne* (2012) remain, as their titles suggest, entranced by Yeats's unrequited love. These studies bring Gonne to us as an abstract idea of an ideal, timeless beauty.[9] *Gonne-Yeats Letters 1893-1938* (1993) and *Too Long a Sacrifice: The Letters of Maud Gonne and John Quinn* (1999), illustrate the extent to which archival resources have been utilised to have frequently served the interests of Yeats scholars, while Sinéad McCoole's *Easter Widows* published during the centenary commemorations, implicitly makes her significance contingent on the execution of her husband, John MacBride. Despite Gonne's efforts to emphasise the significance of her role as a political activist, lecturer and writer in her autobiography and in interviews, the titles of the volumes of published letters on Gonne and the significance of her life and work have frequently been eclipsed by her relationships with prominent, male literary and political figures who played a role in Irish politics of the early twentieth century.

There is no doubt that much of Gonne's impact lay in the power of her famous beauty, which she utilised in her various symbolic roles as the Woman of the Sidhe, the Irish Joan of Arc and, most famously, Cathleen ni Houlihan. The role of Cathleen became a public image after the execution of John MacBride when Gonne took on the role of the endlessly grieving widow, dressed always in a black veil, 'in mourning for Ireland.'[10] The image of Gonne that prevails still echoes the view of William T. Stead who published an article on Irish politics after the death of Parnell. It included a paragraph on Gonne's nationalist activities that concluded: 'although she is hardly likely to be successful where Wolfe Tone failed, her pilgrimage of passion is at least a picturesque incident that relieves the gloom of the political situation.'[11] Yet, ironically, one of the reasons for the relative absence of Gonne from Rising commemorations is because she was deemed such a dangerous political influence in 1916 that the British War office refused to grant her a passport. Little was Stead aware, as he wrote his patronising editorial, that when he first met Gonne in the late 1880s she was undertaking a secret mission to deliver documents to the head of the Holy Synod in St Petersburg for the Boulangiste Party, a venture undertaken for her lover Lucien Millevoye in the interests of their anti-British alliance. Certainly by 1892, Gonne was well known in the press as a prominent Irish nationalist. By

1900, she was under close surveillance by Dublin Castle, having taken a central role in staging a counter demonstration to protest against the Dublin celebration of Queen Victoria's diamond jubilee and the provision of a 'patriotic treat' for children who did not attend Queen Victoria's 'jubilee treat'. She also was known to police through her journalism, notably her incendiary 'Famine Queen' article that resulted in the seizure of all copies of *United Irishman* in which it was published on the grounds that it was treasonous. She also came to the attention of British Prime Minister, Herbert Asquith, on account of her French articles that had been published in the *Figaro*, including 'Atrocités dans les Bagnes Anglais' and the Prime Minister was concerned enough that he asked John Redmond to intervene.[12]

Recently, scholars have emphasised the significance of the nationalist press in the context of the Irish struggle for independence at the turn of the twentieth century. *Maud Gonne's Irish Nationalist Writings 1895–1946* (2004) highlights that Gonne was a prolific and ardent political writer from the 1890s and for the rest of her life, and that, far from removing herself from political life during her self-imposed exile after her separation from John MacBride, she continued to publicise the plight of marginalised, voiceless individuals suffering under British rule, particularly evicted tenants, the Boers, children and prisoners. My own study builds on Steele's volume, examining letters, journalism and the memoirs of her contemporaries to emphasise Gonne's political acumen and the importance of the role she played through the international press.

CHAPTER ONE

The Early Years: A Republican Education

On 21 December 1866 Edith Maud Gonne was born into the affluent household of Thomas and Edith Gonne at Manor House in Tongham, Surrey, as their first child.[1] Two years later, her father, who was a Captain of the 17th Lancers, was appointed Brigade Major of the cavalry in Ireland. Stationed at the Curragh military camp in County Kildare in April 1868, he rented a house in the wealthy suburb of Donnybrook in Dublin for his wife and daughter. The early chapters of *A Servant of the Queen* are filled with affectionate memories of her close relationship with her sister, Kathleen, and their father, who they called by the familiar name 'Tommy'. Tragedy struck the Gonne household when Edith Gonne's precarious health failed her during her third pregnancy; she died in June 1871, shortly after giving birth to her third child, Margaretta Rose, who also died shortly after birth.[2] In the wake of this tragedy, Tommy counselled his children never to be afraid of anything, not even death.[3] Remaining stationed at the Curragh army camp, he secured a house in the Dublin coastal suburb of Howth for his family and their nurse, who educated the two girls in their early years. Much of their time was spent outdoors, roaming the hills of Howth. Gonne adopted the older Irish generation as her own ancestry and recalled visiting 'Granny's cabin'. She always remembered the generosity of families sharing their food with her and Kathleen.[4] The earliest memories Gonne retained from her childhood were of these happy years, and in her interviews and memoirs she always refers to being from Ireland. Gonne traced her family history to County Mayo, as she recorded in a witness statement for the Bureau of Military History, but later stated in her autobiography that, as a republican, she had no interest in tracing genealogies.[5] In *A Servant of the Queen* she makes no effort to establish her own.

Although Tommy had promised Edith he would not send the girls to boarding school or to live with their aunts, his peripatetic military career made this impracticable. When Gonne was six, she and her sister were sent to live with their mother's aunt, Augusta, at Hyde Park Gardens in London. Here, the staid formality of their lives contrasted dramatically with the freedom they had enjoyed on the hills of Howth. However, in 1876 their lives began to change once more as Tommy moved through various military stations in Vienna, Bologna and India. His daughters also travelled, often for the benefit of their health. Gonne's political and social views developed at this time under the tutelage of a French governess, who encouraged them 'to love human beings and to love beauty and to see it everywhere', and taught them history with a republican bias.[6]

Gonne's nascent socio-political views were also influenced at this time through letters from Tommy who wrote affectionately, calling her 'Lamb' because of 'her lovable gentle voice and ways'.[7] In her teenage years, his letters to her show that he treated Maud as an equal as he shared his concerns over the 'cowardly position' of the British forces in Alexandra in 1881.[8] Encouraging the development of an empathetic response to suffering, Tommy sent a guinea to his daughter on her birthday, adding the note: 'Your dad will like to hear how you spent the guinea and hopes that some poor starved creature won't ask for a loaf from his Lamb in vain.'[9] He expressed his fears over the possibility of crop failure and potential famine in

India, asking them to 'say the rain will come'.[10] By the time their father was recalled to work with the British authorities in Dublin Castle in 1882, when Maud was 16 and Kathleen 14, they had enjoyed a liberal education in Ireland, England, France, Switzerland, Belgium and Italy and were both fluent in French.

Tommy died from typhoid fever on 30 November 1886, and the impact of this loss on his 20-year-old daughter permanently embedded the two beliefs he imparted to her at the time of her mother's death: 'You must never be afraid of anything, even of death' and 'will is a strange incalculable force, much more powerful than circumstances.'[11] This belief in channelling will into action, which sounds the keynote of her autobiography, is echoed by her son, Seán, who recorded her conviction: 'Never to be afraid to do something she thought was right.'[12] A providential faith in her cause derived from Tommy, whose childhood portrait she kept until old age. Her daughter-in-law, Kit MacBride, recalled seeing 'tears come into her eyes when she would talk about her father'.[13] The early chapters of *A Servant of the Queen* reflect her loyalty to her father's memory and an attempt to reconcile her father's chosen career with her own beliefs. While stressing the heroism she inherited from her military father, she also takes pains to distance herself from his role in Dublin and the Curragh where he was stationed to keep the peace in the wake of the 1867 Fenian Rising. In *A Servant of the Queen*, Gonne claims that just before his death, on account of the Land War, her father had resolved to resign from the English army and to stand as a Home Rule candidate at the next elections. Reiterating this claim in a witness statement for the Bureau of Military History, she stresses 'We were both so happy when we found our thoughts were as one, for I worshipped my father.'[14] Having to negotiate her political beliefs alongside her emotional connections with loved ones helped her to act according to a thoroughly reasoned-through nationalism. Gonne noted

privately in later years that having her mother's English blood
'makes me able to understand English people and appreciate the
good qualities in them . . . even while my Irish blood obliges me to
fight their government.'[15]

One of Gonne's last references to her father in *A Servant of
the Queen* is her recollection of attending a hunt ball where she
heard the host of the hunting party refer to a man evicted from his
land, whose wife was on the brink of death. The host blamed the
evicted woman's husband for her death and when Gonne protested
that he did nothing to help them, he replied: 'Let her die. These
people must be taught a lesson.'[16] Maud telegrammed Tommy and
asked that a carriage be sent to bring her home the following day.
Although she later claimed to have seen evictions in her early years,
in her autobiography the occasion at the hunt ball is presented as
the defining moment when she turned against her life of privilege.
She recalls of this time of her life: 'I got plenty of dancing, there
were balls and parties every night and it was all such fun but it took
me a long time to discover the war that was in progress, the land
war. I only discovered it when accidentally I saw some evictions
and then I did not want to go abroad or to parties anymore for I
would have had to dance and eat with the victors.'[17] The hunt ball
episode marks a turning point for Gonne. She ultimately had to
choose between the tempting prospects that were open to her as a
wealthy debutante – one who had caught the eye of the Prince of
Wales – and her nationalist political beliefs.

From the point of her father's death, the experiences that
Gonne records indicate preparation for a life of rebellion against
the privileged position which she believed led to the attitude
toward the Irish peasantry that she witnessed at the hunt ball. As
her father died a year and a month before she turned 21 and could
live independently, Gonne and Kathleen remained in London in

the home of their uncle William (their father's sole executor in 1886), until Gonne came of age. William gave them an allowance of 2s 6d a week.[18] Gonne promptly projected her expenses for the month ahead as an amusing act of rebellion against her pedantic and miserly uncle. Perturbed by Gonne's readiness to provide financial support for her father's former lover, Eleanor Robbins, and their illegitimate daughter Eileen, William deceived Gonne and her sister about their own financial expectations, forcing them to draw on their own resources.[19] The episode is an early example of both the feistiness and financial acumen that she demonstrated throughout her life, when she was able to draw down seemingly endless resources as needed.

During her time living in London with her uncle William, Gonne sought means to gain employment. Upon failing a health examination required to practice nursing at Charing Cross Nursing Institute, Gonne contacted the well-known London actor Hermann Vezin with a view to becoming an actress.[20] Devoted to teaching elocution, Vezin honed skills that were to be of service to Gonne throughout her career: speaking on stage, addressing public crowds on lecture tours and in interviews. Contemporaries attested to the power of her oratory and even in old age, her voice has been described as having 'a kind of majesty about it'.[21] However, Gonne was troubled throughout life with respiratory weakness and her acting career was cut short on this account when she was forced to drop out of an English version of *Adrienne Lecouvreur*, in which she had been given the starring role.[22] By this time, in despair that Gonne was bringing shame on the family name, her uncle William admitted that her inheritance would ensure her financial security, freeing her to ultimately turn her oratorical skills to political purposes. Before she did so, a trip to Royat in Auvergne to take the cure for her lungs brought her in contact with another important influence for her future, in its political and personal aspects. It was here that she began her love affair and political alliance with Lucien Millevoye.

Gonne's account of her relationship with Millevoye is notoriously obscure and, as has been often observed, accounts for the difficulties in providing an accurate chronology of her life. In *A Servant of the Queen* she conceals the fact of her 16-year affair with her married lover Millevoye, and the fact that between 1890 and 1894 they had two children: Georges, who died of meningitis in 1891 in France, and Iseult, who survived and returned with her to Ireland. Gonne maintained publicly that she was 'an adopted daughter, or an adopted niece'.[23] Her premonition of 'something tremendous' about to happen in Royat before her meeting with Millevoye, which took place against the backdrop of a spectacular storm, and her sense that she had met him before give what she records as their first encounter a romantic but primarily totemic significance as she casts him as the man who galvanised her to fight for Irish independence.[24] She had, in fact, met Millevoye for the first time before her father's death.[25] When she met Millevoye in Royat he too was there in part for his health, but he was primarily there to collaborate with General Boulanger who led a nationalist movement that sought the restoration of territories to France that had been annexed in 1871 by Germany. At this time Gonne and Millevoye shared an uncompromising nationalist vision. Millevoye promised to help Gonne to free Ireland; in return, she promised to help him to regain Alsace-Lorraine. In a kind of marriage of nationalist ideals, she jubilantly promised 'an alliance against the British Empire' that would be 'a pact to death'.[26]

Leaving Royat, Gonne embarked on an adventurous voyage through Europe, during which time she moved in embassy circles, was believed to be part of a Turkish harem, and at one point, on a brief excursion in a rowing boat in the middle of a ship voyage to

Constantinople, she escaped from a Greek sailor with the aid of a revolver given to her by Millevoye.[27] At Naples she received a telegram from Millevoye asking her to go to Paris where, through his connections, she met Madame Juliette Adam, an advanced nationalist and the mistress of a leading political salon in Paris who had also played a significant role in setting up the French Republic. Adam gave Gonne proposals for a treaty between France and Russia to deliver to Popodonotzeff, head of the Holy Synod in Russia and the Czar's chief adviser. A counterproposal was being sent by the Russian ambassador in Berlin and it was imperative that the treaty papers from France would arrive first. Taking the train to St Petersburg, Gonne sat in a compartment with the documents she was to deliver sewn into her dress: a strategy formerly employed by members of the Ladies' Land League, who concealed copies of the suppressed radical newspaper *United Ireland* in their clothing to smuggle them into Ireland from printing presses in the United Kingdom.[28] However, Gonne encountered a problem on her mission: Russia insisted on passports. At this point Gonne became acquainted with the man whose documents she was to intercept and he was sufficiently impressed with her that he convinced the passport officer to allow her to enter the country without a passport.[29] Jubilantly she records the outcome of this venture: 'In his valise were the very papers from Schuvaloff, Russian ambassador in Berlin, of which Madame Adam had spoken, but hers were delivered first into the hands of grim old Popodonotzeff head of the Holy Synod.'[30] The chapters in which Gonne outlines her adventures around Europe and her first political expedition for the Boulangiste Party reveal a remarkable range of experience for a young woman and a desire for adventure and willingness to take risks in the service of a cause.

CHAPTER TWO

Dublin and Donegal

Once Gonne turned 21 and attained her inheritance in December 1887, she moved to Dublin, staying initially at Airfield with her friend Ida Jameson, a nationalist who had turned against the beliefs of her unionist family. Gonne and Jameson collaborated in the organisation of nationalist cultural activities, on one occasion organising a night of Irish music in which the English national anthem, which was usually played at the conclusion of the night, was replaced with 'Let Erin Remember'.[1] This first public nationalist act, recalled by Gonne with exuberant pride, was one that she claimed was reported in the *Irish Times*.[2] Later, she relocated to the centre of Dublin and from here she sought to join the National League, which was based across the road from her rooms in the Gresham Hotel. However, she was refused membership of the National League on account of her sex. Gonne was then introduced to members of the nationalist Contemporary Club: a liberal, informal gathering of Ireland's cultural elite. Referring to the exclusion of women from nationalist societies like the Celtic Literary Society Gonne records that she 'felt that this Irish anti-feminism was a handicap to the National Movement', and she later established her own nationalist networks for women.[3]

At the meeting rooms of the Contemporary Club Gonne was brought into contact with John O'Leary, the Irish Republican Brotherhood leader; John Francis Taylor, a barrister who represented republican prisoners; and Douglas Hyde, Professor of Modern Irish at Dublin's University College. Witnessing debates representing all shades of opinion, Gonne learned about divisions and factions within the nationalist movement. 'The clash of human intellects is always exciting and sometimes exhilarating,' Gonne wrote as she recalled these debates. 'No two individuals see things from exactly the same angle and if they feel enough and defend their points of view with passion it is like cutting a diamond to make it sparkle with different facets and often throws new light on objects and clarifies thought.'[4] Although Gonne often claimed in interviews that she witnessed evictions in her childhood years, in *A Servant of the Queen* she records this time in Dublin as the time of her education on the scourge of landlordism and political factionalism in Ireland. One of the chief attributes that was to serve her well in the political arena was the ability to understand political dissent and to find points of unity. Her skills in diplomacy seem to have developed at this time under the auspices of the Contemporary Club.

Gonne's increasing association with the Contemporary Club led her to take rooms around the corner in Nassau Street, beside Trinity College. She attempted to learn the Irish language under the tutelage of Hyde, but her reflections on this short-lived effort are an indication of her movement away from cultural nationalism and toward political activism. 'He never succeeded in making me an Irish speaker', she recalled 'any more than I succeeded in making him a revolutionist.'[5] Much of Gonne's time at this point was spent in the National Library, which was located within easy walking distance from Nassau Street. Here, under the guidance of O'Leary, she consolidated her understanding of Irish history and mythology. She met many prominent figures in the Irish Literary Revival although, arriving in Dublin at the end of 1887, she would not yet meet Yeats, who had left Ireland for London earlier that year. Members of the Contemporary Club gathered in Gonne's lodgings and she recalls with pride that 'Many now famous poems and plays had their first reading in those rooms in Nassau Street.' Later, she was to have a momentous impact on Yeats, who was to cast her for the title role Cathleen ni Houlihan in his play of the same name.[6] Such was the impact of her performance when she acted the lead part in *Cathleen ní Houlihan*, a role she played with a 'weird power' in 1902, her miniature was hung on the walls of the Contemporary Club as its presiding spirit.[7] Immersed in the Contemporary Club at this time Gonne was to become a symbolic figure for the associated movement of the Irish Literary Revival. While providing an important locale for the cultural revival, she also recalls of her Nassau Street rooms that 'many plots were hatched in them, plots for plays and plots for real life'.[8]

On her secret mission to deliver proposals for a treaty between France and Russia in St Petersburg Gonne had tasted adventure and she was keen to engage in political action in Ireland. Referring to stories of outwitting the 'G men', members of the Special Branch stationed at her door on Nassau Street, Gonne writes 'the tricks we used to play on those unfortunate sleuths would fill a volume'.[9] Confining herself to illustrative anecdotes she records how she provided stools for the undercover detectives and set up a chase scene 'for exhibition purposes' and how she lead G-men who were following her into a corsetry department.[10] Trivial though these 'little episodes which added colour and gaiety to life' may have been, she drew the attention of the authorities, whose attention she was certainly courting.[11] In an 1890 police report, William Ready referred to her 'histrionic ability' and her 'many efforts to make herself as popular as possible', naming individuals who were frequent visitors to her rooms in Nassau Street.[12]

Gonne's record of the years she spent in Dublin in her 20s gives a sense of the energy, flair for drama and networking skills that aided her later propaganda work. The temperament that led Gonne to play 'chase' with the G-men through the streets of central Dublin prompted her career as an activist and propagandist. One notable example of this was the anti-Jubilee demonstration and the Patriotic Children's Treat she organised on 20 June 1897 to coincide with Wolfe Tone's birthday.[13] She also built up a network of important contacts, including O'Leary, John F. Taylor and Tim Harrington, who invited her to make her first political speech. He also encouraged her to become involved in working in Donegal giving aid to evicted tenants, along with the builder and MP Pat O'Brien. In 1888 she travelled to Donegal with her cousin, May Gonne, to help tenants who were being evicted in large numbers under the threat of battering rams wielded by emergency men, the Royal Irish Constabulary and the military.

Gonne clearly excelled in organising, networking and administrating of practical aid: these were skills that she was to deploy throughout her life campaigning for hungry school children, political prisoners and soldiers wounded in the First World War. Gonne joined forces with the Land League, with support from a central fund overseen by the National League, to build huts for evicted tenants. She recalls how 'boys and girls vied with each other collecting stones for the walls, strong farmers supplied the straw for the thatch, skilled thatchers and masons worked enthusiastically and for love—no one asked pay.'[14] Upon completion of a hut great parties were held that recall the generosity and sense of community she recorded experiencing as a small child in Howth.

Gonne had a talent for building a mythology around herself and she recorded that during the evictions she had been known as 'the woman of the Sidhe'.[15] This appellation invested nationalist mythology with religious fervour as the word *sidhe* was applied in the oldest known Celtic writings to the residences of 'the mystic folk who originally possessed Erinn' who could take on the body of a man or woman and who held out the promise of immortality.[16] Gonne cut an unusual figure in Donegal with her beauty, stature, 'Ascendancy' accent and her large dog, Dagda, named after the god of agriculture, manliness and strength, but she recounts how she gained the trust, even the idolatry, of the evicted tenants she helped. The almost religious worship of her during the evictions that she records in *A Servant of the Queen* was later remembered by her son Seán, who recalled that on a vacation trip to Donegal when he was a child, people kissed his mother's skirts, while Gonne's daughter, Iseult, described her as 'like a live fountain of healing water endowed with a primitive life-giving power.'[17]

But Gonne was not immortal. When she returned to Donegal her lungs deteriorated through the exertion of building huts in cold weather, and her work with evicted tenants was cut short. After nights sitting upright 'fighting against suffocation and coughing little streaks of blood', she realised that she was risking her life.[18] Millevoye, who visited her in Donegal at this time, was gravely concerned for her welfare and argued that she could do much more to further Ireland's cause through propaganda. He suggested that she organise a series of lectures to publicise the evictions and draw attention to the plight of evicted tenants - collecting funds for their support at the same time. Her indecision over whether or not to leave Donegal was ultimately forced to a certain conclusion. In response to the Plan of Campaign, the British colonial administration implemented strident new coercion measures, arresting members of the Land League executive and their supporters. Holding Gonne responsible for undermining the British eviction campaign through her reinstatements of evicted tenants, Wybrants Olpherts, one of the most notorious Donegal landlords, used his influence at Dublin Castle to seek her arrest.[19] Pat O'Brien warned Gonne that she had come under police notice in Donegal and organised for her immediate departure to France via Larne.[20]

Gonne's mission statement from that time, recorded in *A Servant of the Queen*, points to a shift in focus. Although she had to leave through necessity, she saw the wisdom of Millevoye's advice. Before it had come to this crisis Gonne had evaluated what she still wanted to achieve: the release of political prisoners, more time with Millevoye and to begin in earnest 'the fight against the British Empire in international affairs'.[21] She could extend her influence beyond Ireland, working in France for the Irish cause, until such a time when she could return to Ireland under a new government. During a brief hiatus from her work with evicted tenants in Donegal, in June 1890 Gonne entered the public sphere of politics for the first time. At Tim Harrington's behest, she went to the conservative stronghold of Barrow-in-Furness to speak of evictions and Home Rule in support of the Irish candidate, James Duncan. She records that the stage fright that left her speechless was mistaken for excessive emotion brought on by the nature of her subject and she received an ovation.[22] This reaction from the crowd bolstered her faith in her ability to give a spell-binding performance. Once her health was restored, Gonne utilised the contacts she had built up through Millevoye's nationalist circles and channelled her energies into writing a lecture series which she delivered in France. She took lessons in diction from a French actress before delivering a lecture on evictions prepared by Pat O'Brien, accompanied by photographs projected on a 'magic lantern' as evidentiary support.[23] Money collected from the lecture tour was sent to Ireland to help build houses for evicted tenants.[24] Gonne reported that the lectures received great publicity, particularly as women lecturers were rare in those days, and that the illustrated papers reproduced the photographs of the evictions.[25]

Gonne's decision to give a lecture tour to publicise the living conditions of evicted tenants in Donegal was partly motivated by her need to recuperate from her illness abroad in warmer climes, but also because it forged the personal connection with Millevoye that had begun in St Raphael when they were both recovering from illness. Millevoye's nationalism was inspired by Revanchist General Georges Boulanger, who sought revenge over the Franco-Prussian War and the restoration to France of the lost territories of Alsace-Lorraine. In addition to Gonne and Millevoye's own personal alliance, there was a long-held political alliance between Ireland and France. The United Irishmen, founded in the 1790s under the leadership of Wolfe Tone, took inspiration from French republicanism. The French had also provided military assistance to the republican United Irishmen in the 1790s, a historical connection that Gonne emphasised in her lecture tour. Gonne saw an opportunity in the forthcoming centenary celebrations of the 1798 Rebellion to reinforce the close connection between France and Ireland. In doing so, she was able not only to garner attention for the Irish struggle beyond Ireland but to unite conservative and radical nationalists within Ireland in the joint endeavour of commemorating Wolfe Tone with the establishment of nation-wide '98 centennial clubs. According to Arthur Griffith centenary commemorations mark the 'beginning of all modern efforts towards a return to the ideals of independence'.[26] His own contribution, with Gonne's financial backing, was to found the *United Irishman* newspaper, the year after the centenary.

In her lectures in France, while stressing the support that the French had given to Ireland in 1798, Gonne may also have been aware of a more recent alliance between the two countries when, during the Famine and at the time of the 1848 Rebellion in France, Irish republicans had been involved in secret societies in Paris and appropriated many of their ideas.[27] Gonne drew on much that she had learned from the Contemporary Club and her own reading as she developed her lecture series, giving emotive accounts of Irish history with the aim of bolstering French sympathy for the Irish cause. Yeats first met Gonne in 1889, unaware of her relationship with Millevoye. He supported her interest in forging an alliance with France, telling Gonne that he 'wished to become an Irish Victor Hugo'.[28] In later life Yeats admitted to this posturing for Gonne's attention and justified it when he reflected on his comparison, adding 'it was natural to commend myself by a very public talent, for her beauty as I saw it in those days seemed incompatible with private intimate life'.[29] This is perhaps the defensive hindsight wisdom of the rejected suitor, but it echoes the turning point in their lives as they established their different forms of connection with the public. In the 1890s Yeats increasingly took comfort in the seclusion of Lady Gregory's Coole Park estate in Sligo, while Gonne, through her role in the press, emerged as a public figure on the international stage.

From 1889 to 1892, Gonne travelled between France, London and Dublin during a period she describes as one 'of ceaseless activity and travelling'.[30] 1891, in particular, was a tumultuous year for Gonne and one that was to have lasting repercussions, both personal and political. Yeats sensed a deep sadness in Gonne when he visited her in July 1891 after he received a letter in which she described herself as being sold into slavery. Believing her to be in need of 'protection and peace', her sadness prompted him to propose rather than to uncover the cause of her distress.[31] The following month, tragedy struck. Gonne was urgently recalled to Paris where her son Georges had become seriously ill; he died of meningitis at the end of August. Distraught beyond measure, Gonne returned to Dublin on the same boat as that carrying the coffin of Parnell who had died on 6 October, a coincidence that allowed her to cover the much more personal cause of her grief.

After the death of her first baby, Gonne found comfort in her
friendship with Yeats with whom she shared her grief and her belief
in the possibility of reincarnation.[32] To his credit he understood
her need to sublimate her grief through work and tried to direct
her energies to the Young Ireland League, formed in September
1891 at the Rotunda and presided over by John O'Leary. But also,
somewhat desperately, Yeats sought to utilise their shared interest
in the occult, begging George Russell: 'Go and see her when she
gets to Dublin and keep her from forgetting me and occultism.'[33]
In 1891, Gonne joined the Hermetic Order of the Golden Dawn,
which Yeats had joined the previous year. From 1891 their letters
are filled with references to their attempts to communicate on the
astral plane. By 1898 Gonne told Yeats that she had 'seen a vision
of a little temple of heroes which she proposes to build somewhere
in Ireland when '98 is over and to make the centre of our mystical
and literary movement'.[34] Echoing her father's belief in 'incalculable
force' in human will, Gonne reflected back on her interest in the
occult stating: 'I always thought, if there was anything to magic,
well, I would use every force we could for the work.'[35] She believed:
'If I willed I could wish it.'[36]

Although Gonne believed that she could get 'into communion
with the Forces of our country' and direct it toward her work, it is
clear that her interest in the occult could easily be eclipsed by her
involvement with journalism, which was to become her main focus
from this time.[37] In 1900 she wrote to Yeats: 'I intended doing a
little occultism here, but once more I find I am just as hard at work
as I can be writing to America & France about the *U. I.* [*United
Irishman*].'[38] During this time of 'ceaseless activity', she records that
she was involved in 'organising the Amnesty Association in
Scotland and in England; house-building for evicted tenants with
Pat O'Brien in many parts of Ireland; seeing my friends in Dublin;

holding meetings in France and arranging a sort of Press agency for Ireland in Paris.'[39] Gonne's increasing involvement with journalism signals a turning point in her career at the beginning of a decade in which she was to become a founder and editor of nationalist publications and a literary figure in her own right.

CHAPTER THREE

The New Speranza

When William T. Stead met the young radical Gonne on her adventure in St Petersburg, she was still seeking a firm purpose in furthering the Irish cause. He encouraged her to meet Michael Davitt, who had recently published *Leaves from a Prison Diary* (1885), an account of the nine harrowing years he had served in Portland Jail. Davitt had given a detailed description of his treatment in prison before and after his trial to the *Royal Commission Inquiry into the Working of Penal Servitude Acts* from 1878 to 1879.[1] Stead had then commissioned an article from Davitt for the *Pall Mall Gazette* in 1889 to refute Sir William Harcourt's claim that Davitt had ever been in prison for anything other than political causes, and to repudiate Gladstone's statement that his treatment in Portland Prison in 1881-2 was 'in point of decency and indulgence, everything that could reasonably desired'.[2] Gonne was later to take up Davitt's cause of highlighting the unsanitary conditions of prisons and the prevalence of mental health problems for those in solitary confinement, and she campaigned for the recognition of political status for Irish republican prisoners.[3] Davitt became one of the key influences on Gonne's political career even though, unbeknownst to her, when they first met at the House of Commons he had believed her to be a spy, giving her a politely vague response to her query as to what she could do for her country.[4] 'What is this little game?' he wrote on a letter she sent to him, 'Probably a *Times* plot.'[5] Davitt was aware of cases of rich, female provocateurs in Dublin and, on account of its public nature, journalism was the safest medium for Gonne as a new Anglican republican recruit Firm in the belief that 'there is hardly any enterprise in which labour might more readily and withal more usefully engage co-operatively than in running a powerful press', Davitt's suggested that Gonne publicise the evictions abroad.[6]

After her involvement in the Barrow-in-Furness election campaign, Gonne felt that her energies would be better utilised in practical work in Ireland and she concluded that if she ever lectured again it would be in France against the British Empire.[7] In 1892 she undertook this lecture tour, speaking on the evictions she had witnessed. During her time in Dunfanaghy, Gonne had availed herself of the opportunity to speak with a French reporter who had sought to write a first-hand account of Irish evictions for the French press and wanted to test the truth of what was reported in Parliament.[8] In a parliamentary report of April 1889 Labour MP Thomas Sexton recorded a letter from Pat O'Brien on the conduct of the police and the use of the battering ram in evictions. The report concluded with Arthur Balfour's assertion that the battering ram was only used for the purpose of self defence.[9] Gonne gladly enlightened the French reporter, describing a 'one sided battle', with babies born in ditches and 1,000 people evicted and left homeless on the mountains of Donegal in the middle of the winter of 1886.[10]

In France, having a fluent command of the French language and viewing the French as historical allies of the Irish, she could extend the reach of efforts to counter English political propaganda. In her early lectures in Paris she reminded her audiences of General Hoche's efforts to free Ireland from English rule, playing up to French national military pride on every possible public occasion. Chris Healy recalls that she 'began her mission in France by attending every celebration in honour of French commanders, depositing wreaths on their tombs or at the base of their statues, and making eloquent speeches, in which she managed to make reference to England as the hereditary enemy.'[11] Accounts of her lectures attest to the success of her efforts to forge connections between Ireland and France.

In her early lectures in France she also began to build her mythological status for propaganda purposes. Recalling that 'the Maid of Orleans had been burnt by the brutal English', she no doubt used her youth and sex to her advantage by developing an implicit connection with the republican saint.[12] Gonne subsequently published a series of articles entitled 'Le Martyre de l'Irlande', beginning the practice of connecting her individual suffering and martyrdom with that of the nation, which was to be a key element of her propaganda. In doing so within a review of Gonne's lecture tour in France, he linked her with Lady Jane Wilde, who wrote poems and editorials for the newspaper of the Young Irelander movement, edited by Charles Gavan Duffy. This came six months after W. T. Stead summarily dismissed Gonne's contribution to Irish politics in his editorial in *The Review of Reviews*. When an article calling for armed revolution in Ireland was published by Wilde under the name of 'Speranza', the authorities at Dublin Castle shut down the paper and brought the editor to court. Wilde finally claimed responsibility for the article when Duffy refused to name the author. As would become apparent, Yeats's alignment Gonne to Speranza was an apt connection. Gonne was later to relish the opportunity to use sedition and trial to gain further notoriety for an inflammatory article, 'The Famine Queen', published in the *United Irishman* in 1901. Upon publication, the government seized copies of the newspaper, deeming it treasonous.

Gonne adopted the same subject matter and rhetorical effects in her articles as Lady Jane Wilde had in the nationalist poems and editorials that were published in the *Nation*. Depicting vivid images of death in 'The Voice of the Poor', Wilde evoked the horror of the famine of 1847 through the eyes of a witness Likewise, in her lectures and articles, Gonne stressed the visual impact of famine scenes she personally encountered in 1898. Wilde was appointed as a writer in part because the editor of the *Nation* considered her 'the spirit of Irish liberty embodied in a stately and beautiful woman'.[13] However, when Wilde was offered a page devoted to 'feminine contributions', she quipped 'it probably would be the only page left unread'.[14]

In 'The New Speranza', Yeats wrote that 'Miss Maud Gonne is the first who has spoken on the platform wholly and undisguisedly out of a woman's heart', adding that it is the kind of speech that 'could only be made by a woman'.[15] The same is suggested of her writing, as Yeats continues: 'From first to last it is emotional and even poignant, and has that curious power of unconsciously seizing salient incidents which is so distinguishing a mark of the novel writing of women. Its logic is none the less irresistible because it is the logic of the heart.'[16] In attributing Gonne's speeches and writing to her sex, Yeats fails to appreciate the nature of her humanitarianism and the true connection between the two women writers. Gonne, like Wilde, would also focus on nationalist politics over gender politics. Although the *United Irishman* has been described as 'a republican woman studies primer', Gonne's writing is humanitarian rather than feminist.[17] Yeats does her better justice when he notes that her speech has a 'power of seizing upon the distinguishing incidents of an epoch and describing them in vivid and living sentences', and commends a passage in which she gives an account of famine as having the 'serene beauty of good writing'.[18] His account of her speeches also credits her with detailed knowledge of Irish history and an ability to convey the past 'as vividly and simply as if it were all in some famous ballad of "old, unhappy, far-off things, and battles long ago"'.[19] His approbation reflects his own desire to see her as immersed, as he was, in the Celtic Revival. Nonetheless, much of Gonne's journalism is more closely aligned with the 'new journalism' of her contemporaries, concerned with exposing social ills and injustices. This is increasingly characteristic of her later journalism. Thus, Yeats's commendation of Gonne in 'The New Speranza' became tempered in later years with a retrospective view of the differences between them. 'We were seeking different things,' he wrote in his memoirs, 'she, some memorable action for final consecration of her youth, and I, after all, but to discover and communicate a state of being . . . Her two and twenty years had taken some colour, I thought, from French Boulangist adventurers and journalist arrivistes of whom she had seen too much.'[20]

Gonne first established herself as a writer in France where, she noted, 'women did not have the vote but they had great influence in the journalistic world'.[21] In Paris Millevoye introduced Gonne to a number of important contacts for her journalism. Her first article 'Un Peuple Opprimé' ('An Oppressed People') was published in 1892 in *La Revue International*, edited by Madame Ratatzi, a great niece of Napoleon Bonaparte and a contact introduced to her by Millevoye.[22] 'Un Peuple Opprimé' led to a series of articles by Gonne on British oppression in Ireland entitled 'Le Martyre de l'Irlande'; reports which, as Paul Hyland notes, sit somewhat uncomfortably within *Journal des Voyage* in the context of travel writing.[23] To provide a forum more suitable, Gonne founded her own journal, *L'Irlande Libre: Organe de la Colonie Irlandais à Paris* that was, as the title suggested, a much more explicitly political publication. With the help of Ghenia Avril de Saint Croix, a friend made through her Parisian network in the journalistic world, and the secretarial help of Barry O'Delany, Gonne kept the publication in production for 18 issues from 1897 to 1898, with a special issue featuring 'Reine de la Disette' ('The Famine Queen') in May 1897. Resident in Paris when this incendiary article was published, she escaped arrest, which she most surely would have faced if in Dublin

Gonne secured contributions from major figures in the nationalist movement for her new paper. James Connolly wrote on evictions and famine in Kerry, and also on the necessity of socialism in Ireland, Michael Davitt wrote on Anglo-Saxon alliances, while Yeats wrote on the Celtic movement in Ireland. Other contributors wrote biographies of Irish martyrs and articles that emphasised France's association with Ireland in the 1798 Rebellion.[24] 'With this title', Gonne wrote 'the expression of our hopes, we imply the entire programme of our national claims; and it is to France, a land so dear to the oppressed, that we come to pour out this cry for liberty. Moreover, are we not Celts as well, children of the same race, and has not our blood been shed many times on the same battlefields, beneath our allied banners?'[25] As contemporary journalist Chris Healy noted, Gonne's articles figured 'very largely in most of those French newspapers which have distinguished themselves by their furious attacks of Anglophobia'.[26] As a sub-editor's paper *L'Irlande Libre* allowed that any continental paper could re-print its articles and thus Gonne's articles attained an extensive readership of republican sympathisers beyond its immediate circulation.

While French papers reported enthusiastically on her lecture tour in 1892, in England W. T. Stead denounced Gonne for her 'fantastic mission' of founding an association of the Friends of Irish Freedom 'among the descendants of Hoche's Expedition,' which he linked with the damage done to the Irish cause by fanatical devotion to the memory of Charles Stuart Parnell who had died the previous year.[27] Stead's condemnation of Gonne was characteristic of English sentiment toward her as she increasingly courted attention through the press. Gonne was aware that the press in Britain tried to sow seeds of dissent between nationalists in order to weaken the nationalist movement. In 1891 she complained that she was misrepresented in the press: her credentials as a nationalist were called into question by a Mr Teeling, who affirmed he was speaking for the Irish National Party.[28] Gonne refused to respond directly on the grounds that England ruled Ireland by fomenting divisions, citing the result as proof that Irish people are too quarrelsome to govern themselves.[29]

Responding through the pages of the nationalist *Freeman's Journal* Gonne argued that she considered the evicted tenants 'a national responsibility and not a party question' adding that 'in such small efforts as she can make she desires to be kept entirely free from party politics'.[30] In June of 1892 she wrote to the editor of the *Freeman's Journal* to publicise the conditions of evicted tenants living on the meagre allowance from grants from the Plan of Campaign. This allowance had been reduced and, in some cases, never arrived to families 'huddled together in the enforced idleness of the Campaign huts', having no employment opportunities available to them in the district.[31] 'Surely this is no party question,' she concluded, 'but one on which all Irishman should unite'.[32] In her contribution to the ongoing land war, Gonne rose above factionalism, and, through the press, encouraged her readers to unite in support of the poor tenants who, she argued, 'are the victims of English misrule in Ireland'.[33]

Gonne's relentless press campaign against the English focused not only on evicted tenants but on Irish prisoners and their treatment by the British government. Davitt's journalism had an enduring impact on Gonne, who continued to work tirelessly with the Irish National Amnesty Association to campaign for the improvement of prison conditions while highlighting the conditions of prisoners by publishing thousands of articles and notes in English and French papers. Gonne developed an arresting style of writing. With stark detail she documented her own witness accounts of abuses on prisoners, often closing with a rhetorical address implicating not only the British authorities but the Irish for allowing such abuses to continue. An article on the practice of branding prisoners closes: 'How long will the Irish people allow Mulcahy, O'Higgins, and Cosgrave to continue bringing shame on the name of Ireland?'[34] In 'Those Who Are Suffering for Ireland', she sought legal reform as she documented that 'Irish prisoners were convicted almost without evidence and sentenced to penal servitude for life.' 'Where no evidence existed,' she noted, 'the police invented it, going so far as to buy dynamite to plant on persons suspected of being in the Fenian organisation'.[35]

Such a case was brought to Gonne's attention in 1896 when she read that four Irishmen had been arrested in France, Holland and England on charges of planning a terrorist attack. The alleged attack was to take place at the time of the Czar's visit to Paris in September of 1896. One of the alleged conspirators was Patrick Tynan, known as the Number 1 of 'The Invincibles', and his arrest was seen by the British as a chance for retribution for the Fenian dynamite campaign in England. Gonne acknowledged that the men had perhaps been arranging a dynamite plot in England – adding, 'more power to them!' – but said that they were innocent of the plot against the Czar, which she saw as an allegation emanating from England to damage the Irish cause.[36] Gonne read the alleged plot as an attempt by the British Secret Service to draw on the connections made between Fenianism and nihilism in an attempt to derail a proposed alliance between France and Russia.[37] Throughout the 1880s and 1890s, the international press, under the direction of London press agencies, were forging connections between Russian nihilists and Irish-American Fenians. This was a dangerous association that suggested that Irish republicans sought revolution for revolution's sake with no clear goals and no thought to the political aftermath. The Fenian-nihilist connection was one that the British could utilise to their own ends when the opportunity arose.

Gonne read the situation in the context of how the Irish were viewed in the international stage, believing that the Irish cause in France would be ruined if the group of Irishmen were convicted. One of the key figures within Gonne's sphere of influence was nationalist barrister John Francis Taylor and she recruited him to help defend the accused. She also sought Millevoye's aid in preventing the extradition of Tynan, who had been held in France. When Taylor represented Edward Bell at his trial in the Old Bailey in January 1897 information was received that Bell had left Antwerp before the delivery of the explosives took place. The case was readily dropped by the British government, no doubt anxious not to have the attempted stitch-up subjected to scrutiny. Clearly the fall-out proved that Gonne's assessment of the case had been justified. In her autobiography, Gonne records her frustration with how the possibility for a counter-case that would have exposed the British plot was lost. While she commends the effort of a 'well-intentioned Irish back-bencher', namely Pat O'Brien, she notes that he raised the case from the wrong angle.[38] It was claimed that Bell had been arrested merely because he was of Irish origin. Gonne could see that it would have been much more awkward for the British if a British point of view had brought the outcome of the trial into question. She pointed out that an inquiry should have been sought on the grounds that Bell was guilty and remained free. This whole episode shows Gonne's remarkable acuity in reading the political situation (if she is to be believed) and also showed an ability superior to her peers, as to how, potentially, to turn the tables on the British press.

Queen Victoria's 1897 Diamond Jubilee provided an excellent opportunity for Gonne to highlight the plight of evicted tenants.

She did so through a counter demonstration that she helped to stage in the centre of Dublin amid the Jubilee celebrations. Gonne and James Connolly arranged to have the electricity supply to the illuminations on shop fronts cut on O'Connell Street (then Sackville Street), casting it into darkness. Against this darkened backdrop she projected what she referred to as her 'magic lantern show' from a window in the National Club in Rutland Square (now Parnell Square). This show was a projection of images of evicted tenants and the numbers of those who had died on account of British governance of Ireland over the course of Queen Victoria's reign. Gonne's course of reading of Irish history at O'Leary's house and the National Library served her well for the anti-Jubilee protest as she made banners that gave statistics of those who died during the Famine.[39] Greeted with loud cheers Gonne told the crowd that the Queen's reign had brought 'more ruin, misery and death on Ireland than it has suffered during any other period in history', and advised that it was the duty of all Irishmen and Irish women to protest against the 'hateful Jubilee mockery'.[40]

There were four main purposes to the Jubilee counter demonstration and Gonne used the press to follow up for maximum effect. The first was, locally, to undermine the image that the British were presenting of the Queen as bountiful and good to the Irish people, an image that was targeted toward encouraging Irish soldiers to fight for the British in the Boer War. To counter such propaganda Gonne wrote a full article on the abuses suffered by the Irish in Queen Victoria's reign which was published in *l'Irlande Libre* and also in Arthur Griffith's nationalist newspaper, *United Irishman*. In 1900, the *United Irishman* featured a cover image that depicted Queen Victoria as the 'Famine Queen', her portly figure walking past Irish graves which she viewed with a look of disdain, thus undermining the British image projected of Queen Victoria as a loving mother to the Irish nation.

Secondly, the counter demonstration was to highlight internationally the plight of the Irish under British governance. Gonne published a series of photographs of evictions from her magic lantern-show series alongside an article in *Journal des Voyage* for her Parisian readership. Thirdly, it was to ensure that a welcome would not be extended in future years to members of the British royal family. Gonne later played a prominent role in the 'Battle of the Rotunda', when Mayor Tim Harrington was put under pressure at a public meeting to refuse to host a welcome ceremony. The breach of the peace that Gonne instigated was widely reported in the press. In 1901, after the muted response to the Dublin visit of King Edward VII, the American press reported on the consequences of political demonstrations against public displays of welcome for British royalty. The *Irish–American Weekly* reported: 'A national spirit is being developed, and patriotism is being aroused. The Lord Mayor of Dublin accepted a title and made an address to the Queen, and the result was the he was not re-elected. The same thing happened to Major Haggerty, of Cork.'[41]

Fourthly, information about the anti-Jubilee demonstration was circulated to the American press, specifically to seek aid from America at a time when support of the Irish cause was at a low ebb. American newspapers reporting on the Jubilee included the Irish view, noting that placards were held which bore the statement 'During Victoria's reign one and a half millions of people have starved in this island. Three millions have been evicted, and four millions have been compelled to emigrate.'[42] They also commented on the British government's failure to release Irish political prisoners, as had been promised, reporting that one Irish MP concluded: 'It is useless to look further to the English government. We can call upon the voices, and perhaps the arms, of our countrymen in America.'[43]

During this period of Gonne's life, she demonstrated a growing awareness of how to capitalise on the propaganda value of her work with evicted tenants. In 1899, when, an evicted tenant testified in court that Gonne had urged him to take possession of his house and break all the locks, Mr Justice Andrews passed a severe censure on Gonne. With wry awareness of Gonne's ability to manipulate the press, *The Pall Mall Gazette* noted that 'his lordship might have saved himself the trouble, for Maud, who is a sort of Louise Michel of Irish Nationalism, is quite alive to the advantages of a free advertisement. Being always happy to oblige a lady, [the writer notes] the *Pall Mall Gazette* hereby supplements Mr. Justice Andrews by giving her another.'[44] Later that year, wise to Gonne's strategies, the Inspector General reported that, though her activities were seditious, he had decided not to take action as 'it was known that she was only too eager to be prosecuted, in order that she might attain further notoriety.'[45] Rather than continuing to court publicity over individual cases Gonne began to focus now solely on writing articles to publicise the evictions, capitalising on the international attention received over the anti-Jubilee demonstrations.

CHAPTER FOUR

Ireland's Joan of Arc

In 1897 Gonne decided to follow in the footsteps of Irish political prisoners Michael Davitt, John Devoy and James Egan by embarking on a lecture tour of America. Believing Gonne to have 'the genius of the orator',[1] Yeats supported the motion for Gonne's proposed lecture tour in February 1897 and she departed in October for a two-month tour of America, beginning in New York.[2] Gonne's first trip to America was under the auspices of the O'Sullivan section of Clan na Gael, supported by her friend Mark Ryan, leader of the IRB.[3] The tour was primarily for the purpose of raising money for a Wolfe Tone monument for the centenary commemoration of the 1798 Rebellion and for the Amnesty Association for political prisoners. She also planned to invite delegates from America to Ireland for the 1798 commemorations. Furthermore, one of Gonne's primary objectives at this time was to launch a counter-propaganda campaign in America. In 1897, in an interview published in *The Irish Standard*, Gonne complained

> England has press agents. Ireland is alive with them. She sends bogus dispatches to the newspapers, tending to show that the majority of the Irish people are not in favour of a change; that the nation is dormant and quite regardless of a feeling of liberty. I am also connected with a news agency, and its intention is to forestall the false reports sent out by England's staff.[4]

That the American press reported so enthusiastically on Gonne's arrival in New York on 27 October 1897 suggests that a considerable amount of preparation went in to laying the groundwork for her media campaign in advance of her departure. Her first lecture was delivered to an audience of nearly 1,000 people and at the peak of her hectic two-month tour she drew crowds of up to 3,000 people.[5] When Davitt, Devoy, Parnell and Egan lectured in America, reports indicated that they lacked the charismatic appeal later attributed by the press to Gonne in their enthusiastic responses to her lecture tours.[6] A practised speaker by this time, Gonne drew on her dramatic training and also her experience at the Barrow-in-Furness by-election. The *New York Times* reported that her voice quivered with emotion and faltered several times, suggesting that, through an emotional performance, she sought to reproduce the powerful effect of the speech she made during the Barrow-in-Furness campaign.[7] Gonne's clothing drew much attention, with reporters recording that she wore a bullet that she claimed was picked up by a child in the fields of Castlebar when French officers helped 1,000 Irish put 5,000 English to flight.[8] In reports on interviews Gonne's birthplace changes to suit the occasion, one newspaper reporting that she was born in Kerry,[9] while in other interviews, she was happy to have the American press use the fact of her English heritage, as this made her anti-English sentiment more rhetorically powerful.[10] However, one consistent image emerges over the course of the American tour: Gonne was cast as an Irish Joan of Arc, committed to the cause of her homeland – an image that took firm hold in the American press.

Newspaper articles from Gonne's tour each have a slightly different origin for the moniker 'Joan of Arc' as it was applied to Gonne, some claiming that this was how she was known in France, and others claiming that this was how she was known by the Irish peasantry.[11] Reports of Gonne's lectures suggest that she was trained in oratory, perhaps under the tutelage of Taylor, her close associate whom Gonne considered to be the finest Irish orator of his time.[12] Taylor also wrote a monograph about Joan of Arc. Gonne's rhetoric appealed to American sentiment with one reporter stating: 'The Irish Joan of Arc found in the present condition of Ireland a counterpart to the condition of the colonies just before the revolution.' On this occasion, Gonne read portions of the Declaration of Independence to highlight this fact and then cried: 'Do not these noble words apply to us? Our only remedy is what yours was.'[13] Gonne also presented herself in the less militant role of the new woman journalist. She clearly led interviewers in the manner in which she wanted to be depicted. The *San Francisco Call* recorded: 'The beautiful patriot is a distinctly modern product. She believes firmly in the axiom, "The pen is mightier than the sword" and it is to the press and the lecture-platform that she looks to for the liberation of Ireland rather than to deeds of physical prowess.'[14]

While Gonne's lecture tour raised £1,000 for Clan na Gael, her skills in diplomacy may also have eased political tensions in Irish-American organisations at a time of great factionism in Irish politics. Gonne's visit to America was during a time of crisis within Clan na Gael following the formation of an extreme militant branch-off group that caused many Irish Americans to withdraw financial support from the Irish cause.[15] There had also been another split in Clan na Gael that Gonne believed was on account of the British Secret Service having spies in both camps to maintain division in Irish-American organisations. This split emerged when a Dr Cronin, who was going to give evidence to the Times Commission, was found dead. Alexander O'Sullivan, one of the leaders of Clan na Gael, was accused of having instigated the murder. After her lectures in America Gonne appealed to the two sides to resolve the split, urging them to rise above their differences, which were only serving the interests of the Empire.[16] One American paper, *The Irish Standard*, suggested that, although being 'somewhat handi- apped' by being managed by one organisation, she contributed to a rapprochement of divided factions of nationalists in America.[17] While it may be that this report of Gonne's unifying influence rested on nothing more than her own opinion, her ability to speak for the cause rather than the faction, which was the defining feature of her political activities, was exactly what was needed at this point. By 1901 Clan na Gael was united once again.

Gonne's visit to America in 1897 came at a crucial time in both Irish-American and Anglo-American relations. Launching *L'Irlande Libre* in 1897 Gonne had considered the political significance of the Irish diaspora, and in particular the 'seven million Irish in America' who have 'more than once blocked English diplomatic moves'.[18] Gonne was reflecting on this at a crucial time when, after half a century of disputation, England and America sought to reach agreement over a major arbitration treaty, namely the Olney-Pauncefote Treaty of 1897. Fearing that America would become a catspaw for England Gonne addressed the issue during her lecture tour of that year. Giving the principal address to a large gathering in Chicago in November 1897, Gonne urged Irish-Americans to oppose ratification of the Treaty.[19] England wanted the treaty, Gonne said, 'not for peace, but to bolster her war prestige else-where.'[20] M. V. Ganlon, who was presiding over the Chicago lecture, closed proceedings by condemning the proposed treaty and calling upon all men of Irish blood to oppose it.[21] Michael Davitt and John Devoy also travelled to America that year specifically to oppose the treaty. The ultimate outcome was the rejection of the treaty, with at least 23 of the 36 petitions opposing ratification coming from Irish-American organisations such as those that Gonne, Davitt and Devoy addressed.[22]

When Gonne made another visit to America in January of 1900, $1,000 was raised in advance of her arrival.[23] According to one source, this second visit was to 'urge her countrymen to rise in revolt against England while Great Britain is engaged in South Africa.'[24] Gonne fulfilled all of her engagements during the tour, which she said was to 'cement the unity of Irish sentiment in Ireland and America' and prevent enlistment, but this time, a hectic lecturing schedule led to ill-health.[25] 1900 was a difficult year for Gonne; in a poignant letter to Yeats she reflected on how she had dealt with her grief over the death of her son, Georges: 'I have chosen a life which to some might be hard, but which to me is the only one possible. I am not unhappy only supremely indifferent to all that is not my work or my friends. One cannot go through what I went through & have any personal human life left . . . what is quite natural & right for me is not natural or right for one who has still his natural life to live.'[26] Yeats was not always able to act toward Gonne in a way that put her interests first, but on learning of the death of her son he understood her need to throw herself more fully into her work. By 1900 this work was largely concerned with journalism and propaganda. Yeats supported her journalistic campaign in his article 'The Freedom of the Press in Ireland' in which he entreated readers to carefully watch Lord Cadogan and his government as they had ransacked newsagents and railway trains to suppress Gonne's *L'Irlande Libre* and *The United Irishman*.[27] Yeats had asked John O'Leary to encourage Gonne to work for the Young Ireland League because she needed 'some work of that kind in which she could lose herself'. She was, Yeats noted, 'enthusiastic about the League'.[28]

Gonne's involvement with the Young Ireland League brought her into contact with Arthur Griffith, a young journalist and editor, who approached her in 1899 with Willie Rooney, founder of the Celtic Literary Society, to ask her to support the *United Irishman*. This began as a half-penny weekly that held an 'ideal of an independent Irish republic uniting all its people regardless of their religion'.[29] Within a year it grew to an eight-page penny weekly distributed by agents in Belfast, London, Paris, New York, Brooklyn, and Philadelphia, a rapid expansion that can be attributed to Gonne's skills in networking.[30] Relationships forged on her American tour (notably Joseph Smith), as well as those she knew through Millevoye in France, were vital for the distribution of the paper.[31] Gonne also held an important role in overseeing its content. Frequently it was used to promote her activities, reporting on her work on evictions in Mayo and advertising her attendance at commemorations of former nationalist uprisings.[32] The success of the *United Irishman* depended on the high profile of contributors, including W. B. Yeats, J. B. Yeats, J. M. Synge, Michael Davitt, John O'Leary, James Connolly, Anna Johnston and Alice Milligan, all personally known to Gonne. Gonne also contributed her byline to the paper. Alice Milligan, editor of the *Shan Van Vocht*, noted that women could 'transcend the political schisms which divided male groups, as well as organising more freely than their male counterparts, who might be carefully watched by the police.'[33] One arena in which women could play an important role was through journalism. The feminist-leaning *United Irishman*, which gave women a political voice, became closely associated with Gonne's new venture, a women's nationalist organisation – Inghinidhe na hÉireann – that she inaugurated on 10 April, 1900.[34]

CHAPTER FIVE

Inghinidhe na hÉireann

Finding herself excluded from membership of nationalist organisations on account of her sex Gonne gathered a meeting at the Celtic Literary Society offices of about 15 sisters and girlfriends of her nationalist friends, known to her through the Contemporary Club and Young Ireland Society.[1] They formed the group Inghinidhe na hÉireann (Daughters of Ireland) as the 'Woman's Organisation for the Independence of Ireland' and elected Gonne as president.[2] Establishing themselves in the rooms of the Celtic Literary Society, members of Inghinidhe na hÉireann adopted Gaelic names (to anonymise the writing of those who worked for Unionist firms) and they established the National Purpose Fund to support ventures designed to combat English influence.[3] The goals of Inghinidhe na hÉireann were 'to support and popularise Irish Manufacture, to discourage the circulation of English literature and Newspapers, the singing of Irish songs, attending about all English Entertainments at the Theatres and Music Halls and to combat English influence in every direction.'[4] Inspired by the work of the Celtic League, Inghinidhe na hÉireann's manifesto was to be 'a women's national society for the advancement of the Irish language, literature, history and industries specially amongst the young.'[5]

One of the key missions of Inghinidhe na hÉireann was to influence young children and protect them against English influence, or, in Gonne's words, 'to undo the work that the enemy was doing in Ireland'.[6] Recalling the focus of their work in an interview in 1937, Gonne recalled 'England was trying to Anglicise our children, and forbid certain subjects in the schools.'[7] To counteract the effects of an English educational programme, Inghinidhe na hÉireann offered free classes in Irish history, language, music and dancing. One of the first events they organised was a direct response to a propaganda exercise organised by the British government to bolster support for the monarchy and to lay the groundwork for the British army's campaign to recruit Irish soldiers. The 'Patriotic Children's Treat', held in Clonturk Park in Drumcondra on 1 July 1900, was a reward for those children who had not attended the 'loyal treat' given by Queen Victoria. Addressing the children, Gonne asked the boys to keep their patriotism as pure and bright and glorious as it was that day, and never let themselves be tempted to join the English army, navy, or police.[8] Reporting on the event, the *United Irishman* supplanted Queen Victoria with Ireland (or Gonne) as Queen, appearing as the Patriotic Children's Queen 'not as the Shan Van Vocht, "the mother of exiles", waiting for the children who have gone, but as Kathleen the Beautiful, bright with hope, and powerful with the wonderful vitality of the Irish race.'[9]

Through the pages of the *United Irishman*, Gonne congratulated and thanked the children who she believed had 'done more for the Irish cause than all the meetings which have been held and all the resolutions which have been passed for many a long year.'[10] The politicisation of children continued annually with a 'Christmas treat' when the provision of cakes, sweets and minerals was accompanied by magic lantern pictures illustrating the effects of British rule in Ireland and abroad.[11] Under the direction of their Inghinidhe na hÉireann teachers, children pledged never to enlist in the English army or navy.[12] National Boys' Brigades, established to prevent enlisting, were supported by generous subscription from the Ancient Order of Hibernians American Alliance.[13] The

mission of Inghinidhe na hÉireann was foundational and long
term in its agenda; its membership urged, under the direction of
Gonne, to 'Remember that the children today are the men and
women of tomorrow.'[14]

Gonne was duly proud of the achievements of Inghinidhe na
hÉireann, particularly as its members were working in an anti-
feminist atmosphere that had precluded women from joining a
political society. Within this atmosphere they embraced the chal-
lenging task of influencing men, often doing so indirectly, charging
women not to consort with soldiers. They also directly addressed
young men, distributing anti-listing hand bills and publishing
articles urging Irishmen against enlisting in the British army. In 1901
Gonne quoted statistics showing that the Irish element in the British
army had fallen from 35,000 to 23,000, which she credited to the anti-
recruitment campaign.[15] One of the distributors of anti-recruitment
pamphlets, Helena Moloney, recalled how

> This campaign led to a prolonged newspaper controversy which
> showered us with abuse and called us all sorts of names, and we
> individually got a constant supply of anonymous letters of the foulest
> nature. It was not pleasant, but it did raise a volume of opinion.'[16]

While subject to some hostility as Moloney notes – the 'ninnies'
as they were sometimes called – minimised the criticism levelled at
them by limiting their agenda to the nationalist cause, and were
thus 'unique amongst women's associations in that [they] took no
interest whatever in women's rights or suffrage – just [doing] what
was most urgent for Ireland.'[17] Suffrage was debated in Westminster
and Inghinidhe na hÉireann held that 'the feminist cause in Ireland
is best served by ignoring England and English politicians.'[18]

In a decade in which many Irish newspaper editors were taken
into custody on charges of sedition, Gonne's support of a nationalist

newspaper and establishment of a nationalist organisation were public activities that brought her further scrutiny. On 7 April 1900, Dublin Castle police descended on the offices of the *United Irishman* to seize all copies containing what they deemed to be 'a seditious publication calculated to produce discontent and disaffection amongst her Majesty's subjects which appeared in that week's issue.'[19] Gonne, who had signed the article 'Miss Maud Gonne', was in France and so avoided arrest. In 1900, part of the fall out from the publication of Gonne's 'Famine Queen' article was that she was accused in the pages of the *Irish Figaro* of being a spy in receipt of a pension from the English government. Editor and director of the *Irish Figaro*, Ramsay Colles, was accused of printing, publishing and circulating 'scandalous and malicious libel' that was 'calculated to lead to a breach of the peace'.[20] Arthur Griffith had rushed to Gonne's defence, breaking his whip in the process of administering a physical assault on Colles. The court case that followed forced Gonne to clarify her position as an Irish nationalist of English birth. In a lecture on 14 October – entitled 'Irishmen and the English Army' – Gonne definitively clarified her position: 'Her father was a unionist Home Ruler, and wanted Home Rule for Ireland and a Parliament in College-green, but he wished Ireland to remain united with England – a part of the Empire. She was a separatist.'[21] She relished the publicity she received from the Colles trial, buying a new hat for the occasion and was delighted when excerpts from 'The Famine Queen' article were read aloud in court as evidence against her, only giving her views wider circulation.[22]

In the aftermath of the publication of 'The Famine Queen', Gonne made a brief and ill-fated attempt to rally support for the Irish cause in England. At a meeting in Liverpool, the police were forced to disperse the crowd, some of whom were intent on making 'a mess' of Gonne and her friends, and a lady who was mistaken for

Maud Gonne, the Irish Joan of Arc, equipped to help the Boers, 1901

National Archives, Kew, CO 904/202 (1)

Gonne was mauled by the crowd.[23] The following year a satirical image of Gonne was published under the heading 'Cranks and Freaks of Today, Feb 1901', featuring her as she was imagined to have appeared at the opening of 1889 when she declared allegiance to the Boer cause.

The image of Gonne dressed in military costume with the features of a Huguenot is labelled 'The so-called "Irish Joan of Arc"' alongside claims that she never departed for South Africa as it was claimed she would, because, it said, 'There was metal more attractive in the United States via Funds.'[24] The leaflet was circulated during her American tour of 1901 as it noted 'Maud is still passing the hat around in New York at this date (Feb 1901)'. In addition to accusations of self-promotion, the final line even sought to undermine the otherwise unquestioned fact of her great beauty, claiming 'she is not a beauty but oh! Gosh!', so that the overall effect was to denigrate her as a fraudulent, attention-seeking and ugly 'new woman'.

Although never actively militant like her Inghinidhe na hÉireann protégé Constance Markievicz, Gonne frequently advocated physical violence as the only remedy against British oppression. On one occasion when Gonne lectured in France in 1892 to rallying cries of 'Long Live Ireland!—Long Live France!', the event was rounded off by poetry recited by French soldier-poet Lucien Gillain, and in the following year, Gonne wrote a preface to his volume of poetry entitled *Heures de Guerite*, subtitled 'Poems of a Dragoon':

> From out of the depths of the abyss, the Unhappy Ones glimpse a star which shines in the sky: it is that of France, homeland to all those who wish to see their country free. And that is why the Irishwoman sends you this testimony of her lively sympathy and her wishes for the victory of your cause.

May Alsace and Lorraine become French again!

May France remain great in order, because of the weight of its generous efforts, to influence the destinies of the world.

May she

With all the vanquished against all the tyrants

bring about the triumph of this principle of natural justice and eternal right: 'it is up to all nations to determine their own fate!'[25]

In December 1889 Gonne had written to Yeats expressing her regret that he had not written a poem against the Boer War as he had planned.[26] As if, in part, to renounce Yeats, in her preface she addresses Gillain: 'In your country, the poet is a soldier, and poetry is a prayer to God for your country' and the headpiece for the volume features an illustration of a uniformed soldier and Maud Gonne.[27] But Gonne's faith in French support was soon to wane. In *A Servant of the Queen* Gonne records that Millevoye published an article in his newspaper, *La Patrie*, that identified Germany as the one and only enemy of France and demonstrated that he ultimately supported the 'Entente Cordiale' between France and England.[28] This article had been penned by an opera singer who was likely to have been his new lover. Gonne's account of the betrayal focuses on the fact that she had encouraged him to take up editorship of the paper in the aftermath of Boulanger's death. Gonne records that she put her

> whole will into making him regain confidence in himself and realise that, with his wonderful power of literary expression, he would be able to make that little-read paper an instrument with which to rebuild the shattered fortunes of his party and regain his old influence.[29]

Under Millevoye's editorship, she noted, *La Patrie* had become 'one of the most influential of the Paris newspapers'.[30] Their alliance, which had primarily centred around their mutual support of each other's journalism, ended at a time when Gonne was at her most militant. She had even advanced plans to sink a ship of British soldiers on their way to the Transvaal by loading bombs disguised as lumps of coal on board one of their ships. When her plans were undermined by a British agent, who secured £2,000 from his uncovering of the operation, Gonne made no further attempts in espionage or militant exploits.[31]

Despite her plans for physical force activity at this time Gonne was always treated with some suspicion by the IRB; even when she befriended its leader, Mark Ryan, her role was as one of the 'paymasters of all Irish separatist endeavours', a key element of this being her funding of the nationalist paper, *United Ireland*.[32] As with Davitt, it is likely that Ryan only trusted her in the publically visible role as propagandist. Chided by Millevoye as he censured 'would-be revolutionists playing at revolution', Gonne left the IRB and began a new political and romantic alliance, this time with Irish war hero John MacBride.[33]

John MacBride was a native of Mayo, a county badly affected by evictions and claimed by Gonne in the 1920s as the home of her ancestors. Like Gonne, MacBride was a person of interest at Dublin Castle, and he recalled how by 1895 he 'could not go anywhere without having a brace of detectives on [his] heels'.[34] He distinguished himself fighting on the side of the Boers against the British in the Transvaal and had founded the Irish Transvaal Brigade for soldiers fighting on behalf of the Boers against the English. When the Irish brigade disbanded MacBride went to France where he met his former war comrade, Arthur Griffith, and through him he met Gonne who was then living in Paris. Gonne had been a founding member of the Irish Transvaal Committee, had held a pro-Boer rally in October 1899 to launch an anti-recruitment campaign to deter Irishmen from enlisting to fight against the

Boers, and arranged French passports for Irishmen going to join the Irish Brigade.[35] MacBride was a man of action whose reason for leaving the Transvaal was that he wished, according to Gonne, 'to take a hand in things in Ireland'.[36] Gonne saw MacBride as a potential propaganda tool and considered him as having 'done more for Ireland's honour than all of us at home, for it is action that counts'.[37] To her, he was a man who had 'saved Ireland's honour at a time when there was a great need'.[38]

Living primarily in Paris from 1900, where she was listed in the city directory as a 'publiciste', Gonne turned to MacBride for help with her propaganda work.[39] She sought to bolster his public status, establishing the MacBride club in Dublin, and used his example to deter enlistment of Irish soldiers in the British army. In April 1900, Gonne's 'Famine Queen' article lauded the Boers for destroying the illusion of England's war prestige. After a failed campaign to enter politics as an independent in the 1900 South Mayo by-election, MacBride was in need of employment and Gonne encouraged him to take up journalism to help with the anti-enlistment campaign.[40] In a letter published in the *Mayo News* MacBride wrote 'urging Irishmen to prevent any recruits joining the British Army, and asserting that the British Empire was a blood-sucking vampire, and that the Nationalist representatives in Parliament wanted to send Irishmen to France and Belgium and leave their bones in foreign countries, and that dying Catholic soldiers in France had no chance of receiving the Sacraments.'[41]

Griffith and Gonne asked MacBride to embark on a tour of America to lecture on his military service for the Boers as leader of the Irish Transvaal Brigade.[42] In 1895 MacBride had represented the nationalist group the Irish National Association at a convention in Chicago but he was not skilled in oratory as was necessary for an extended lecture tour. Lacking Gonne's charisma and criticised for reading from notes MacBride received little press coverage during his American tour in 1901 and ultimately, at his request, Gonne joined him, taking over the role of lecturer to raise money, dually, for the *United Irishman* and the widows and orphans of Boer soldiers. On this lecture tour, Gonne was at her most militant as a speaker, declaring that Irish freedom could be secured only by force of arms 'which she frankly advocated.'[43] On receiving a letter from Griffith that she was badly needed in Dublin, Gonne left MacBride in America hoping that he 'might succeed in setting the match to the inflammable fighting forces of the *Clan na Gael*.'[44] This was to be Gonne's final lecture tour of America. Although reports of the tour point to its success, with John MacBride recording that 2,000 were turned away from their lecture in Boston, Gonne returned to Ireland where she redoubled her propaganda campaign with Inghinidhe na hEireann, which in October 1900 had affiliated with Cumann na nGaedheal.[45] This linked up all existing nationalist societies into an open separatist movement.

On her return to Dublin in May 1901, Gonne turned her attention to the Irish National Theatre. Her dramatic training with Hermann Vezin led her to take a leading position teaching drama with Inghinidhe na hEireann, which led in turn to her working with well-known Dublin theatre producers Frank and Willie Fay. They produced tableaux vivant of scenes from Irish history, in part to supplement the income from the National Purpose Fund.[46] Alice Milligan and Anna Johnson helped to stage the society's tableaux and, as their ambitions and confidence grew, they developed plays drawing on the same emblematic representations of Ireland as a woman that they had represented in their 'signature tableu', 'Erin Fettered and Erin Free'.[47] This featured Inghinidhe na hÉireann actresses in the role of Erin, first kneeling at the foot of a cross in chains and ending with her 'standing triumphant and holding off the shining sword', with religious and military imagery that was to become central to such tableaux and

later, to National Theatre plays.[48] After witnessing the performance
of Alice Milligan's *The Deliverance of Red Hugh*, which was produced by Inghininde na hÉireann, Yeats recalled: 'I came away
with my head on fire.'[49] As Senia Pašeta notes: 'The early activities
of the Inghinidhe foreshadowed this nascent dramatic movement,
with the most committed members planning from its first days to
establish the nucleus of a national dramatic company which would
run in conjunction with Nationalist organisations in the city.'[50]

   In 1899 Gonne acted as a financial guarantor for the Irish
Literary Theatre formed by Yeats, Lady Gregory and Edward
Martyn.[51] When the Abbey opened in 1904, Ireland had, for the
first time, a national arena for the staging of Irish drama, with
performances by Máire Nic Shiubhlaigh, Sara Allgood, and Maire
O'Neill, whose talents had been fostered by Gonne.[52] As President
of the National Players Society, Gonne worked with Arthur
Griffith and Edward Martyn toward cultivating nationalist drama,
which culminated in 'A Great Week of National Plays' in October
1905. Throughout these crucial years that witnessed the birth of
the Irish Literary Theatre, Yeats and Gonne had worked closely
together. While Yeats recorded their first meeting as the occasion
when 'the troubling of his life started', Gonne's chief concern had
been with how the young poet could help her to publicise the
evictions she had just witnessed as she turned her attention to a
counter-propaganda campaign.[53] The culmination of her request
for Yeats's help was a play that he would only give to Inghinidhe na
hÉireann on the condition that Gonne would play the title role.
This play was to become a piece of iconic nationalist propaganda,
Cathleen ni Houlihan.

   As a key symbolic figure of apogee of the Celtic Revival, which
culminated in the prolific output of the Irish Literary Theatre,
Gonne was acutely aware of the power of mythology and its role in
political activism. She may also have been aware of how she was

viewed as a symbol by Yeats, whose memoirs record a reflection that begins 'Thinking of [Maud Gonne], as I do, as in a sense Ireland, a summing up in one mind of what is best in the romantic political Ireland of my youth.'[54] When Yeats first met Gonne he beheld in her 'the classical impersonation of the Spring,' noting 'the Virgilian commendation "She walks like a goddess"' was 'made for her alone'.[55] Building on the 'Woman of the Sidhe' mythology that had centred around Gonne in Donegal, Lady Gregory and Yeats co-wrote the one-act play, which features a peasant family who, when preparing for a wedding, receive a visit from an old lady. The play ends with a visitor being asked if he has seen an old lady on the road, to which he replies, 'I did not, but I saw a young girl, and she had the walk of a Queen.'[56] Gonne played the title role to a packed audience, recorded by a reviewer as being 'largely composed of Miss Gonne's ultra-nationalist following'.[57] Christopher Morash noted that she arrived ten minutes before the curtain went up, 'unprofessionally (but impressively) sweeping through the audience in full spectral costume as the Poor Old Woman' to connect with the audience in the context of a formal theatrical performance, bringing some of the unexpectedness and dramatic flair characteristic of her later activism.[58]

Prior to Gonne's debut in *Cathleen ni Houlihan*, Yeats had been concerned about the success of the play, but Máire Comerford later recorded that '[h]e need never have been under any illusion as to its effect on the young people who saw it. 'Never did a great poet ever have actors to interpret him who were so involved personally as the girls of "Inginidhe na hEireann" – Maire Nic Shiubhlaigh, Maire T. Quinn, Sarah Allgood, and the incomparable Maud Gonne.'[59] Comerford stated that '[t]he appeal of Ireland, depicted as a poor old woman, claimed and has had, the service of my life' and she linked the transfiguration of Gonne that night to the transformation of Irish politics.[60] 'In the audience that same night, or during the season', she noted, there must have been men and women who soon would take part in the Irish Revolution. Roger Casement might have been there, with Alice Stopford Green, Art O'Brien, future representative in London of the first Dáil Éireann, Sorcha MacDermott and Cis Sheehan of Cumann na mBan, the last two my friends in jail afterwards, or Fintan Murphy, who helped in de Valera's escape from Lincoln Jail in 1919.'[61]

Cathleen ni Houlihan 'had such a success', Gonne recalled, 'that when we wanted to renew our contract at the end of the week for the Hall, it was taken from us under the excuse that we were blocking the traffic; so many people had to be turned away every night.'[62]

Audiences were so transfixed by the 'weird power' of Gonne's enactment of woman-as-nation and the emotive force of the metaphor of the rejuvenation of the country through the blood of young men that reviewer Stephen Gwynn wrote that 'the effect of "Cathleen ni Houlihan" on me was that I went home asking myself if such plays should be produced unless one was prepared for people to go out to shoot and be shot.'[63] Although after 1916, Yeats famously asked 'Did that play of mine send out/ Certain men the English shot?' he later distanced himself from his influence on the rebellion, shifting responsibility to Gonne in his 1916 poem 'No Second Troy'. In this, he claimed that Gonne 'taught to ignorant men most violent ways'.[64]

While the impact of the play on men has been well documented, less has been said about the significance of the play on its female audience and on their political involvement in the Rising. By literally placing women centre stage, *Cathleen ni Houlihan* galvanised to action a number of members of Inghinidhe na hÉireann whose participation in the nationalist movement was electrifyingly represented by Maud Gonne; Máire Comerford, for example, recorded: 'The play that mattered was "Kathleen ni Houlihan". That night my fate was sealed, my course in life set in the direction it was to take.'[65] She also noted the pervasive impact of the play on her contemporaries, noting that 'Helena Molony, a founder member, and Maeve Cavanagh MacDowell went on to join the Irish Citizen Army; Elizabeth O'Farrell and Julia Grennan, who distinguished themselves as dispatch carriers from the GPO in Easter Week, 1916 had both been with Inghinidhe in the Audience at the first performance of *Cathleen ni Houlihan* in 1902.'[66]

Yeats's views on Gonne's impact may be accounted for not only by the power of her performance but also her own, more militant literary contribution to the National Theatre and Literary Revival after her success as Cathleen. In 1904 Gonne wrote *Dawn*, a one-act play with three tableaux, which was published in *United Irishman* in 1904.[67] As with Yeats's play, a female protagonist represents mother Ireland, but while Yeats had shied away from religious imagery, following accusations of heresy in response to *The Countess Cathleen*, *Dawn* draws much more extensively than *Cathleen ni Houlihan* on nationalist 'Rising' imagery, presented as an image of a sunburst in one of the three Fenian flags used in the Easter Rising.[68] *Dawn* is an explicit call to arms as Bride, the play's heroine, advocates a militant response to the practice of evictions. Gonne may have found her inspiration for the play in Lady Jane Wilde's poem 'The Dawn', which offers a mystical vision as thousands 'gather in might' with a banner 'traced in the heart's blood', which 'flings out in flame-words – Liberty and Right!'[69] The title of Gonne's play, *Dawn*, and its three tableaux, 'sunset, night and dawn', are linked with the rising of violent sentiment which intensifies over the course of the play into a resolve to rise up against 'the Stranger' and reclaim the land that has been stolen. Rejecting the possibility of availing of external aid from America, on the grounds that 'those who go far come back too late', the female figure of Bride says to her dying daughter Brideen: 'The river of blood must flow, but there is freedom on the other side of it, and the Strangers are driven away like clouds before the sun. Brideen, it is you and the mighty dead who are driving back the clouds.'[70] Gonne saw the death toll of war as a necessary evil, as 'through the smoke, and the fire, and the darkness, life, light and regeneration will come.'[71]

For the setting of *Dawn*, which takes place at an undisclosed location at 'a ruined, roofless cottage by the roadside on the edge of a bog', Gonne drew on her own experience of famine exacerbated by evictions in Belmullet and the scourge of relief works, which she documented in her journalism from 1898 to 1900.[72] Here, Fr Munelly told Gonne the prophecy of Brian Ruadh: 'That there would be a famine and a woman dressed in green would come and preach the revolt. After that, many men would rise and there would be fighting and many killed but that the English would in the end be driven out.'[73] According to the legend, Brian Ruadh died the day after he wrote down his prophecy. Gonne's play merges the prophecy with her own role as 'Woman of the Sidhe'/ 'woman dressed in green' in the roles of Brideen, whose death prompts her mother Bride (the spelling of the name echoing MacBride) to prophecy the 'red dawn' of war as the only remedy to drive Strangers from their land.[74] The red dawn, symbolism with which the play closes, is explicitly linked with the image of the 'river of blood' that is deemed necessary to attain freedom. Although considered an imitation of *Cathleen ni Houlihan*, Gonne uses powerful radical 'Rising' imagery as a much more central trope to *Dawn*, with Ella Young writing a lyric 'The Red Sunrise' for it.[75] Gonne understood that the power of *Cathleen ni Houlihan* came from her performance of the title role and the mythology that grew around her. Although there is no indication that she intended to cast herself for a role in a performance of *Dawn*,

Gonne invoked one of her favourite images of the mythical 'Queen' with reference to the character 'Bride':

> Old Michael: Bride, Bride of the Sorrows, it is your service I took. I have been faithful. I thought one time I might have been one of the stones your foot would rest on when you walked to Freedom – when you will drive the Stranger out – but I am too little a stone.
> Bride: Michael you have served him, and you will serve me.
> Old Michael: Only one of the little stones which keep her feet from sinking in the soft bog, till she drives the Stranger from her fields. There are many little stones that the feet of the Queen have rested on shining out across the bog.[76]

While in *Cathleen ni Houlihan*, suffering is implicit in the fact of the old woman having lost her land to the stranger, *Dawn* points directly to the effects of the stranger's actions with explicit reference to starvation and the condition of the works system. While the power of Yeats's play resides in its mysticism, the force of *Dawn* lies in its realism, as it draws on Gonne's personal experience of famine and evictions in Belmullet. Such force was more successfully delivered through Gonne's journalism, in which she invited the readers to share the shock of the vision she encountered in Belmullet in 1898 through a powerful first-person narrative account:

> How few people realise what the distress in the West really means! [. . .] I know I did not understand it when last week I gaily mounted a car at Ballina for the forty miles' drive into Belmullet, and now seated comfortably in the train wrapped in furs, with a good footwarmer, looking out on the green fields on my way back to Dublin, the remembrance of those crowds of famished creatures, whose ragged

garments fluttering in the wild Atlantic wind scarcely hid their gaunt limbs, and whose blue lips implored help, seems already to me like some terrible nightmare vision.[77]

The difference between *Cathleen ni Houlihan* and *Dawn* reflects the ideological conflict between Yeats and Gonne over the cultural role of art. Yeats's later regret over his literary contribution to the nationalist sentiment that culminated in the 1916 Easter Rising expresses the tension, by then largely resolved, between his desire to please Gonne by furthering her cause and his wish to extricate himself as an artist from politics. *Cathleen ni Houlihan* was, in fact, billed in Dublin for Easter week 1916, but it was not performed.[78] As Yeats increasingly held to the 'art for art's sake' manifesto of the modernist movement that he shared with Lady Gregory, Gonne held to the 'art for propaganda' side of the debate.[79] She regretted the influence of Lady Gregory on Yeats, which meant 'no more poems against English kings' visits'.[80] She would later deeply resent Synge's depiction of the Irish in *Playboy of the Western World* (1907), relating to John Quinn: 'I heard French people say "If the Irish peasants are such drunken besotted creatures as that, England does well to oppress them."'[81] When *Dawn* was published in October 1904, the leading figures in the Irish theatre movement were focused on the imminent opening of the Abbey Theatre, but in September 1903 Gonne had resigned from her role as vice president because of in-fighting among the Irish theatre movement, explaining to Yeats: 'I won't undertake any but National fights, & the theatre Co does not seem inclined for such fights.'[82] The play thus only appeared in print in *United Irishman* and now alongside Gonne's journalism in Karen Steele's *Maud Gonne's Nationalist Writings 1895–1946*.

CHAPTER SIX

Maud Gonne MacBride

With its religious symbolism of resurrection and salvation, *Dawn* accommodated the enormous influence wielded by the Catholic Church. The influence of the Church was also a factor Gonne had to consider in her journalism. Lady Gregory once observed to Gonne: 'All our country is for Parnell . . . but they will probably vote with the priests.'[1] From the time of her earliest eviction work in Donegal Gonne was aware that the majority of priests would not condone violent resistance to the authorities, and in the 1898 famine in Mayo she found people reluctant to steal in order to survive due to an entrenched Catholic morality. In response, she collaborated with James Connolly in 1898 to produce the pamphlet 'The Right to Life and the Rights of Property', which justified stealing on the plea of necessity as sanctioned by Pope Clement I, Pope Gregory the Great, Thomas Aquinas and Cardinal Manning.[2]

Gonne's close friend, Eileen O'Brien, referred to her as 'deeply religious', but Gonne's initial conversion to Catholicism was no doubt to distance herself publicly from her English heritage and to further her political agenda.[3] Gonne found that propaganda against her frequently referred to the fact of her English parentage and birthplace. Even O'Brien saw Gonne as 'part of the ascendancy', noting that 'she would have come in under [the generic title] of the ascendancy because she was part English.'[4] In June 1902, when Gonne accepted John MacBride's proposal, she announced in a letter to her sister: '1st I am to become Catholic, 2nd I am to get married to Major John MacBride, this last is not public yet.'[5] Her conversion to Catholicism *was* a public act. She explained to Yeats: 'I prefer to look at the truth through the same prism as my country people – I am going to become a Catholic . . . I do feel it important *not* to belong to the Church of England.'[6] Predictably devastated, Yeats pragmatically argued against her marrying MacBride in terms of her own argument on religion, stating that it would 'do great injury to the religeon [*sic*] of free souls that is growing up in Ireland, it may be to enlighten the whole world.'[7] Undeterred by friends and family who begged her not to go ahead with the marriage for the sake of her future happiness, Gonne took religious instruction from Canon Dissard, a friend of her former lover, Millevoye. Dissard was 'a fervent Nationalist whose hero was Napoleon', who she first met at a meeting of Boulangist friends at Royat in the early 1890s.[8] He encouraged her conversion to the faith of the Irish people, and in her account of her conversion, Gonne recalls that he attributed her desire to become Catholic to 'ancestral memories'.[9]

Dissard overcame her concerns over the doctrine of papal infallibility, on account of the Pope condemning the Plan of Campaign in Ireland during the Land Wars. He argued that the Pope was not infallible on political matters, adding: 'God has never promised immortality to nations and leaves to the people the responsibility of holding the land he has given them, and, if they don't do so, they deserve the misery that comes to them.'[10] He also alluded to the fallibility of the French bishops who burnt Joan of Arc.[11] Having overcome these difficulties Gonne was keen to publicise her decision to convert to the faith of her adopted country. In *A Servant of the Queen*, the propaganda value of the conversion is disguised as Gonne presents her conversion as less of a political manoeuvre by making it fit with her narrative that subordinates her will to a mystical destiny in a chapter entitled 'The Inevitability of the Church'. Nonetheless, her conversion was a public declaration of her allegiance to the nationalist cause and linked to her high-profile marriage. When Gonne was officially received into the Catholic Church at the Carmelite Convent of Laval on 17 February 1903, she took the name of her future mother-in-law, Honoria.[12]

Four days after her confirmation, Father Van Hecke, the former chaplain to the Transvaal Brigade, acted as celebrant for the marriage of Maud Gonne and John MacBride in the Church of Saint-Honoré d'Eylau in Paris. The best man carried the flag of the Irish Transvaal Brigade while the bridesmaid bore the blue flag of Inghinidhe na hÉireann.[13] The wedding ceremony, which concluded with a toast to the 'complete independence of Ireland', has been aptly described by Roy Foster as 'a new form of political theatre'.[14] But for Gonne it was also intended to be a genuine new political alliance. In MacBride Gonne found the possibility of a new alliance with a military hero at a time when she was at her most militant. She married him, she claimed, so that she would 'be able to more effectively serve the cause of independence'.[15]

Their marriage was to begin with the assassination of Edward VII in Gibraltar, where they had planned their honeymoon to coincide with the King's visit. Gonne claimed that the attack did not happen because MacBride was drunk, but, as Ward notes, the dates of the honeymoon in Gibraltar did not coincide with the royal visit.[16] Gonne revealed to a friend that on her wedding night her husband had come to her 'footloose drunk' and that the honeymoon in Spain had been a 'disaster' because of his drinking.[17] As with her planned dynamite campaign, the proposed assassination was exposed. An insider revealed the plan in an anonymous letter to police in 1903, adding that Gonne ought to be in an asylum.[18] The press capitalised on Gonne's mistake, spreading the rumour that she was operating as a double agent, giving information on Irish nationalists to the authorities of Dublin Castle.[19]

From the time of her confirmation and marriage, Gonne sought opportunities to use her new-found Catholicism for propaganda. When King Edward VII was to visit Ireland in 1903, Gonne sought to expose the fiction circulating in advance of the visit that the king was 'secretly a convert to the Catholic religion and has deep affection for his Catholic subjects'.[20] The Bill of Rights 1688 required the monarch to make a solemn public declaration of non-belief in the Roman Catholic faith. This read: 'the Invocation or Adoration of the Virgin Mary or any other Saint, and the Sacrifice of the Mass, as they are now used in the Church of Rome, are Superstitious and Idolatrous.'[21] Gonne ordered 10,000 copies of the Coronation Oath printed on handbills to draw attention to the anti-Catholic sentiment of the oath and she instructed Inghinidhe na hÉireann to have them posted throughout the capital. Gonne noted that the handbills presented the authorities with a difficult problem: 'They could not call the Coronation Oath seditious literature,' she noted, 'and they dare not arrest us for it.'[22] Arrests, she knew, would only draw attention to their campaign and bolster their own propaganda.

Gonne was disappointed in what was eventually merely a muted response to King Edward's visit to Dublin.[23] Determined to garner the kind of attention she had enjoyed in the Battle of the Rotunda Gonne staged her own protest at her home in Coulson Avenue.[24] Utilising the occasion of Pope Leo XIII's death on 20 July for a display of Catholicism, Gonne mounted a black petticoat on a broom handle to contrast with the flags set out for the royal visit. When she sent word to Inghinidhe na hÉireann that she needed back-up, the protest escalated into a stand-off that involved her wielding a fake gun. Gonne had been disappointed not to have had a public demonstration against the royal visit such as she had orchestrated in 1897 and characteristically made up for it by getting the most propaganda value out of this impromptu protest that she could. The 'Battle of Coulson Avenue', as she styled it, drew the attention of press correspondents from foreign newspapers who were in Dublin to report on the royal visit, giving Gonne the opportunity of explaining the significance of refusal of a civic welcome to the anti-Catholic Edward VII with a display of mourning for Pope XIII.[25] It was in actions such as this 'siege' that Gonne's unflinching confidence and charisma drew her supporters and built the incipient women's movement within Irish nationalism.[26]

This 'siege', clearly a favourite of her anecdotes in *A Servant of the Queen*, earned Gonne congratulatory telegrams from Paris from John MacBride and W. B. Yeats, but it also led to an important friendship with Helena Molony. Molony was recruited to Inghinidhe na hÉireann on the day of the battle of Coulson Avenue and   later served with the Citizen Army during Easter Week.[27] In 1908 Inghinidhe na hÉireann established a monthly journal which was edited by Molony and published by Gonne. Entitled *Bean na hÉireann* (The Woman of Ireland), the masthead echoed the dawn image of Gonne's play, featuring a woman standing before a rising sun holding the title banner of the paper.

Marrying John MacBride and thus becoming part of a high-profile nationalist couple with plans for physical force action did not deter Gonne from her propaganda campaign. Two weeks before their marriage, in an article entitled 'The Irish Press', Gonne deployed military language as she urged her readership to keep the Irish press 'bright and sharp and keen, like the sword of the Gael and following the true tradition and mission of the sword which is to inspire as well as defend.'[28]

Having established MacBride as a journalist, Gonne wrote to Kathleen in her letter about their proposed marriage: 'Of course he has no money, but he earns his living as a journalist and I think we'll always get on.'[29] But the marriage ended in acrimony, Gonne accusing her husband of drunkenness and criminal assault; he, perturbed by her confession of having been 'the mistress of three different men', accusing her of 'a complete lack of all womanly delicacy' and 'constant lying'.[30] One of the contentions in the divorce suit concerned Gonne's claims that MacBride was financially dependent on her because of his failure as a journalist.[31] MacBride's primary occupation after his marriage was as a secretary to Victor Collins who was correspondent to the New York *Sun* and Laffan's Bureau, a news agency in New York.[32] Perhaps MacBride's most enduring contribution to Irish politics was that the nationalist movement would adopt a motto of 'Sinn Féin' ('Ourselves') to describe their objectives.[33] In the separation hearing Gonne's lawyer stated that MacBride was 'an illiterate man who was only capable of making rough translations for the papers'.[34] MacBride's defence counsel argued that the marriage was a sham and that Gonne had used 'the military glory of the Major' as part of the political game she was playing in the press.[35] Having made him a media figure for nationalist propaganda she lamented the squandered opportunity. Merely a year after the marriage ceremony she wrote to Yeats: 'Of a hero I had made, nothing remains & the disillusionment is cruel.'[36]

The dissolution of the marriage was a test for this seasoned propagandist. Despite her conversion to Catholicism prior to her marriage to MacBride, Gonne sought a full divorce that would be permitted on the grounds of her charges of immorality and drunkenness, considered 'L'injure Grâve' in the French courts.[37] Clan na Gael opposed the suit, believing that the Irish cause would be hurt if a patriot as well known as MacBride were forced to undergo the humiliation of a public divorce.[38] However, MacBride had friends in the press. His former employer *The Sun* used the imminent canonisation of Joan of Arc as an occasion for lambasting Gonne as a Catholic woman in the divorce courts:

> Over in Paris Maud Gonne MacBride is suing her husband for divorce. In chronicling the case the cable perpetually refers to her as 'The Irish Joan of Arc.' Emphatically and distinctly it is time to abandon that foolish appellation. [. . .]
>
> Joan of Arc was an earnest, practical Catholic. Maud Gonne was not.
>
> Joan of Arc led the arms of her country and gained phenomenal victories. Maud Gonne has never done so.
>
> Joan of Arc never took her woes into a divorce court. Maud Gonne has done so.
>
> Joan of Arc was a heroine as well as an uncanonised saint. We want some sensible citizen to show us one heroic action Maud Gonne has ever done.
>
> It is folly, sheer nonsense in fact, to be advertising the divorce court lady as a person heroic and reverent as one whom the Catholic Church is about to declare a saint. The great Celtic race is not so badly in need of heroines that it must accept Maud Gonne.[39]

The 'divorce court lady', who was not 'a persona grata' even in the more liberal social world of Paris, felt the weight of Catholic Dublin public opinion when, accompanied by Yeats, she attended the Abbey premier of *Deirdre*, *The Gaol Gate* and *The Mineral Workers* in October 1906.[40] She was hissed at by the audience, and Annie Horniman viciously stated afterwards that 'Mrs. MacBride got what she deserved'.[41] Gonne smiled tolerantly through the public show of scorn at the Abbey, but the consequences of her separation were significant, especially, as *The Sun* article demonstrated, because the success of her propaganda rested on her public image. Ironically, the media show of her marriage to MacBride ended in a propaganda battle with her husband that risked undermining everything she had worked for as a public figure. John MacBride filed suit in Dublin against the *Independent*, accusing them of publishing libellous information.[42] The metaphor of warfare that Gonne had applied to her personal war with England was now one that she applied to her marriage and the custody of their son, Seán. She wrote to Yeats of 'fighting an uneven battle because I am fighting a man without honour or scruples who is sheltering himself & his vices behind the Nationalist cause.'[43]

The aftermath of the separation had been foreseen by Barry O'Brien who had earlier advised MacBride to avoid all public recriminations of Gonne as they had publicly identified as a married couple in parallel with the Irish cause, and 'any scandal arising from public recriminations might reflect injuriously on [their] country.'[44] Likewise, when Gonne had considered pursuing the case in Ireland, O'Brien cautioned her:

> This is no ordinary case of difference between husband and wife . . . this is a case in which Irish national considerations must be taken into account. Therefore I cannot regard with indifference the prospect of seeing you and your husband made the subjects of ridicule and contempt by the press of this country.[45]

The advice was prescient. Many years later, Senator Michael Yeats declared that for the sake of posterity he would ask for letters about the divorce to be suppressed, noting that it was 'a very nasty case [and] would do harm to a dead hero and his living family if published.'[46] Pilloried in the press Gonne resolved not to respond: 'The judgment in the court,' she decided, 'will be sufficient answer'.[47] The outcome of the divorce suit, which was heard in front of a small audience chiefly composed of members of the bar on 27 July 1905 was that because MacBride succeeded in proving Irish nationality and domicile, 'only separation [and] not divorce could be granted'.[48] Under the terms of the separation Gonne secured guardianship of Seán, which had been her chief concern, and following the outcome of the trial MacBride returned to Ireland with Gonne remaining in Paris.[49] Having changed her name on her marriage to Maud Gonne MacBride, she reverted to her maiden name, 'Gonne (Mme Maud)' in the directory where she was listed as residing in 17 Rue de l'Annonciation, which was to be her primary residence until 1916.[50]

From 1906 Gonne spent most of her time in Paris, wishing to keep Seán away from his father and English law 'until he is old enough to defy both'.[51] Previously exiled from Ireland as a soldier who had fought against the English, MacBride was now able to return to Ireland under the general amnesty after the South African War. When Yeats asked a fellow club member why MacBride's presence in Ireland was suddenly tolerated, he was told: 'That is simple; it will keep Maud Gonne out of Ireland.'[52] Nonetheless, Gonne tolerated public scorn and made regular visits to Ireland after her separation, leaving Iseult and Seán under the care of her friend Mme Avril de Ste Croix.[53]

In Dublin Gonne continued to publicise the issues closest to her heart, concerning the welfare of evicted tenants, prisoners and children in Ireland. When it came to providing practical aid, she was incredibly pragmatic and forward-thinking. During her time in Mayo at the time of the 1898 commemorations Gonne had witnessed famine conditions and she adopted an inventive strategy of developing plans for fish-curing in Belderrig, County Mayo, to provide an alternative staple food source to the potato.[54] In the first decade of the twentieth century, she steered a school meals initiative based on Canticus Scolaires model in France to address what she saw as the British 'famine policy' being applied to children.[55] When the scheme was rolled out to every school in Dublin, her work was commended by the Chief Health Officer of Dublin, Sir Charles Cameron.[56]

In the wake of her separation Gonne immersed herself in the therapeutic occupation of painting. In 1910, she illustrated Ella Young's *Celtic Wonder Tales*, a collection of Celtic myths for children, dedicated 'to Seaghan, Iseult and the Pirate and to the Sacred Land'.[57] While the politicisation of children through educating them in their ancient history had always been an important aspect of her work since she established Inghinidhe na hÉireann, Gonne was also fundamentally concerned with their health and welfare, particularly in the context of the poverty she witnessed in the early years of the twentieth century. At the time of the Children's Patriotic Treat, Gonne expressed her belief in her own generation's duty to free Ireland for her children, but at times she felt it would be a task passed on to the next generation.[58] At the end of 1910 she wrote to Quinn: 'This neglect of the children – It is one of the most vital natural questions, if we are to get free & keep free we must keep up the strength of the race & *compulsory* education & compulsory starvation is sapping it.'[59]

While primarily resident in France, she returned regularly to Dublin in the first decade of the century, closely following debates over the prospect of Ireland at least attaining Home Rule. She expressed her love of Dublin to Quinn, noting hopefully that 'Ireland is so interesting just now.'[60] Two years later, however, she wrote, 'Dublin is very sad just now. The misery is bad [and] is getting worse every day.'[61] This was during the strike and Lockout which began in Dublin in August of 1913. Alert to the problems inherent in the strike action Gonne noted that while the union men involved in the Lockout received support from Britain, those who never thought of striking but were unable to work due to a general stopping of trade would receive no strike pay and would starve as a result.[62] At this time she sold a diamond necklace, her last item of jewellery, in order to pay for school dinners for children.[63]

While she objected to what she saw as an obscure prejudice against socialism in Ireland, Gonne never aligned herself directly with any party or political 'ism' in Irish politics other than nationalism.[64] The suffering she witnessed in Dublin at the time of the Lockout changed her political outlook. While she had confirmed her position as a separatist in 1900, by 1913 she would have accepted Home Rule to remedy the grievances of the urban workforce.[65] When war broke out in August the following year she viewed it as an 'inconceivable madness' with 'no great idea behind it'.[66] Characteristically, although she lamented France's involvement as a nation, her focus was on how ordinary people would suffer the most, noting upon the outbreak of the war that it would most affect those countries that had conscription.[67] Also characteristically her thoughts turned to the effect that the war would have on the Irish cause. In 1914, despondent that the outbreak of the war did not lead to independence, she wrote 'My only hope is in Home Rule. I feel that bad as that bill is, it will cheer us all up a bit, put us in a better position to get more,' although Quinn believed that a broader measure of self government would be attained after the war.[68]

Upon her return to France in March 1911 Gonne published articles about the poverty she had witnessed in Dublin and forwarded money sent by Quinn from America to continue supporting relief work in Ireland.[69] When Inghinidhe na hÉireann evolved to become Cumann na mBan in 1913, Gonne held the role of honorary president from France, where she continued to write articles for *Bean na hÉireann* and also for the trade union weekly *The Irish Worker*. She lamented that Irish employers were starving strikers into submission during the Lockout, blaming the fact that they were protected by a British-controlled legal system.[70]

In July of 1914, when war had seemed to be ever imminent, Gonne hoped that the question of Irish independence would be resolved at last and that the British need for Irish support would result in Redmond securing a great deal for Ireland.[71] She wrote to John Quinn: 'I am very low-spirited about this war and think more than ever that *peace* is the only thing worth striving for – but how to work for it is what I do not know.'[72] Distressed by the suffering she witnessed Gonne volunteered as a nurse with the Red Cross at Argelis. When her exceptional organisational skills were recognised, she was transferred to the Paris-Plage where she nursed soldiers who had been sent directly from the front. Working tirelessly administering aid she recorded that 'We certainly saved several lives not so much by nursing as by supplying proper food.'[73]

But her concerns with the war were bound up with her fears for Ireland. She was disappointed with the Home Rule bill that was put through parliament in September of that year, as it would not take effect until after the war and Ulster was to remain under British rule. On 26 August 1914 she lamented to Yeats that 'Redmond seems to have wasted a glorious opportunity & Ireland seems too confused & inarticulate to redeem his mistake.'[74] On 7 November 1915, Gonne recounted in a letter to Yeats a strange dream she had:

> I have been seeing, I think I have been among, Masses of spirits of those who have been killed in this war, and they are being marshalled & drawn together by waves of rhythmic music [. . .] It is leading them back to the spiritual Ireland from which they have wandered [and] where they would find their self realisation [and] perfectionment [and] to whom they would bring their strength.[75]

This was no doubt influenced by the Great War, but was also strangely premonitory.

CHAPTER SEVEN

The Rising and After

In February 1916, while nursing the wounded in France, 'patching up poor, mangled, wounded creatures in order that they may be sent back again to the slaughter', Gonne began to consider relocating to America, believing that Europe would not be fit to live in for generations.[1] Two months later, the news arrived of the failed military insurrection in Dublin and the arrest of its leaders and John MacBride. Although he attended a meeting of the Supreme Council of the Irish Republican Brotherhood in 1914 to plan a military operation against British rule, MacBride had not been a leader of the Rising and in fact he stumbled upon it by accident. Nonetheless, drawing on his military leadership skills he took control of Jacob's factory.[2] In his trial MacBride willingly admitted his role as second in command, adding that he could have left Jacob's factory before the need for surrender, however he considered it a dishonourable thing to do.[3] On account of his prominence in the action, MacBride was one of the 16 men to be executed in the uncompromising reprisals for what was deemed to be a treasonous uprising. Desperate to return to Dublin when she first heard news of the insurrection, Gonne was unable to secure a passport. In the aftermath of the Rising Yeats visited her in France. Geraldine Dillon, sister of Joseph Plunkett, recalled being there when Yeats proposed to Gonne again and that her father had to bring a 'hysterical' Maud home.[4] Insensitive to the complexity of her response to her husband's death, Yeats reacted with some bitterness to her unfaltering rejection of him and was unsympathetic to her as she tried to return to Ireland, noting that 'Maud Gonne will certainly do something wild,' in league with Constance Markievicz if she returned to Dublin.[5] Although ill-tempered in tone, Yeats was probably correct in his assessment that 'the authorities do not want to have two such mad women on the loose in Ireland'[6] and he spoke bitterly to Ezra Pound of her 'pure and disinterested love of mischief, or of a row'.[7] He did ultimately help her to secure a passport the following year, but all Gonne could do in 1916 was send money to Ireland to relieve the distress of the families of those who had been arrested and sent to prison camps in England.[8]

Overwhelmed with sorrow for the loss of her friends, Gonne assuaged her grief through her belief that 'practically & politically their sacrifice will avail'.[9] While Quinn assiduously contacted representatives of the British Embassy, emphasising that it would be diplomatically expedient to spare Casement and the leaders of the Rising from execution, Gonne worked to counter and forestall negative press accounts of the events of the Rising.[10] The British press were quick to report on the suppression of the insurrection and made reference to Irish support of the British military response, quoting letters from Irish people that called for the harshest reprisals. Defending his leadership as Chief Secretary of Ireland at the same time that he resigned from the post, Augustus Birrell stated in Parliament on 3 May 1916:

> This is no Irish rebellion. I hope that, although put down, as it is being put down, as it must be put down, it will be so put down, with such success and with such courage, and yet at the same time humanity, displayed towards the dupes, the rank and file, led astray by their leaders, that this insurrection in Ireland will never, even in the minds

and memories of that people, be associated with their past rebellions, or become an historical landmark in their history.[11]

As time would reveal, the British administration had entirely misjudged public sentiment.

While Gonne sought to defend the memories of those who had given their lives in the Rising – many of them personal friends – she also forestalled false accounts of her husband's death. She wrote to Quinn:

> It is characteristic of the English to insult a fallen adversary – the *Daily Mail*, Paris Edition, announcing his execution had an article full of lies which I had to contradict in the French press. I could not bring myself to write to an English paper.[12]

A rumour had circulated that MacBride had refused the assistance of a priest in his last days before he was executed. Quinn requested an accurate account from Father Augustine who had given MacBride counsel and administered the sacraments to him in his final days.[13] Father Augustine was keen to dispel such a rumour, writing to Gonne that he had seen an account of his last moments in an English paper which was 'purely imaginary'.[14] He revealed that he was with MacBride until his death, and that when offered a blindfold he had replied 'I have looked into the barrels of guns too often to be afraid of them now. Fire away!'[15] She immediately viewed MacBride's death as an honourable sacrifice for the nation and wrote with pride: 'My husband is among those executed – He and MacDonagh gave themselves up from Jacob's biscuit factory to save the civil population of that crowded district – from indiscriminate shelling by the English, he has died for Ireland & his son will bear an honoured name. I remember nothing else.'[16]

Viewing MacBride's death as a sacrifice that overwhelmingly undid the wrongs she personally had experienced at his hands, she resumed using the name 'Maud Gonne MacBride', only choosing to use the French term of address 'Madame' rather than 'Mrs' to reflect that the affiliation was not a marital one.[17]

In the wake of her husband's execution, Gonne expressed her wish to Quinn that she could 'get named Dublin correspondent to some well-known American newspapers', noting that 'with Ireland under [martial] law it is most necessary.'[18] She gave an interview from Paris to the American newspaper *The Sun* (MacBride's former employer), as the French press was unsympathetic to her on account of the war-time alliance between Britain and France.[19] Her article appeared in a full-page spread on 16 July 1916. In this interview, in which she is again Ireland's 'Joan of Arc' emphasising the religious mission behind the cause, Gonne aligned herself with her husband from whom she had been estranged for twelve years, elevating the executed rebels to a saintly status, referring to them as 'Apostles of Liberty'. She also gave an impassioned plea for Home Rule, referring to England's need to wipe the stain of their fresh blood from her hands before she went into the peace congress as a champion of liberty and of small nations. Appealing to Quinn for an inquest into the British military response to the Rising, she noted that 'The Americans have had committees looking into the charges read against the Germans in Belgium . . . could not Irish Americans get such a committee appointed to look into the charges made against England in Ireland?'[20] 'Such support,' she argued 'would be of immense moral value to Ireland & would perhaps, shame the English into settling the Irish question', adding that 'It would also be of historical value as showing the sincerity of the champion of small nations.'[21] Although Gonne asked Quinn, who supplied her with articles from American press, to secure her a position as a correspondent, Quinn's primary concern at this point was winning the war against Germany.[22]

Gonne felt the need to counter reports that were circulated not only in the British press, but also in the depiction of John MacBride given by Yeats in his poem 'Easter 1916', in lines that referred to him as 'A drunken, vain-glorious lout'.[23] Although characteristically polite in all her letters, Gonne launched into a letter to Yeats: 'No, I don't like your poem, it isn't worthy of you & above all it isn't worthy of its subject . . . As for my husband he has entered eternity by the great door of sacrifice . . . so that praying for him I can also ask for his prayers.'[24] She added: 'You who have studied philosophy & know something of history know quite well that sacrifice has never yet turned a heart to stone though it has immortalised many & through it alone mankind can rise to God.'[25] For Gonne, MacBride's death elevated him to the status of those leaders such as Tone and Emmett, whose images adorned the walls of Irish cottages she visited and that were revered alongside religious figures. Yeats's poem did nothing to elevate the status of the rebels into martyrs. She later wrote to Quinn that she liked James Stephens's poem on the uprising in Dublin better than 'Willie's "Easter 1916"', which she considered 'inadequate for the occasion'.[26] Stephens's *Green Branches* collection, published late in 1916, evokes the same imagery that was prominent throughout Gonne's propaganda campaign:

> Now we are resurrected, now are we,
> Who lay so long beneath an icy hand,
> New-risen into life and liberty,
> Because the Spring is come into our land.[27]

Resurrection symbolism combined with a military conception of nature would have appealed to Gonne much more than Yeats's heart of stone. Two years later Gonne was making 'allegorical pictures of a spotless infant' representing Ireland.[28] Even in her final years she spoke 'in pseudo-mystic terms about Ireland, the great trilogy as she called it, of blood and soil and spirit'.[29]

After months of appealing her case, Gonne decided to accept the limited conditions that would allow her to journey to England but not Ireland, with no guarantee if she left France that she would be allowed to go back.[30] Arriving in Southampton in September 1917 she was served with the Defence of the Realm Act, disbarring her from travelling to Ireland. By evading the surveillance of two CID men and leaving Turkish baths in disguise, she ultimately managed to escape from London, where she had stayed with Eva Gore-Booth.[31] Leaving Iseult in London she returned to Dublin where she stayed initially with Constance Markievicz before securing a house at St Stephen's Green.[32] It was judged by the Chief Secretary that Gonne should not be taken notice of as long as she 'behaved reasonably'.[33] The Dublin Metropolitan Police monitored her activities throughout the next five months, during which time she protested against the export of food from Ireland and against the forcible feeding of political prisoners. She also was involved in events organised by Sinn Féin, the Irish Citizen Army, and the Socialist Party, and caused the authorities concern by maintaining regular contact with Constance Markievicz.[34]

In 1918, as a high-profile nationalist and 'a person suspected of acting, having acted, and being about to act in a manner prejudicial to the public safety and the defence of the Realm', Gonne was targeted in what became known as 'The German Plot.'[35] When a former member of Roger Casement's brigade was arrested after he landed from a German boat in County Clare, he claimed the Germans were planning to send a military expedition to Ireland. Lord French, recently drafted in as Lord Lieutenant of Ireland, released a proclamation on 18 May 1918 alleging a conspiracy between Sinn Féin and the German Empire to start an armed insurrection in Ireland. The Dublin Castle Executive was persuaded to arrest practically the entire Sinn Féin leadership on warrants issued under the Defence of the Realm Act and they were held in English jails on the night of 17 May. Most of the arrests were deemed 'preventative', the official position being that 'trouble was likely, and that it was better to lock up a certain number of people than to have a lot more shot, and a few more in danger of hanging.'[36] On 19 May 1918 Gonne was taken into custody in the police station in Dublin Castle, and the following day she was sent to England where she was interned in Holloway 'for the duration' along with Countess Constance Markievicz and Kathleen Clarke.[37] Although the rationale for her imprisonment was questioned in a parliamentary debate on the grounds that she had been in France 'during almost the whole period of the story of the so-called German plot', Mr Bonar Law responded tartly that 'Almost does not cover the whole time'.[38]

For Markievicz, imprisonment was an advantage that bolstered her status and helped her, while in jail, to secure electoral victory – a victory that has been described as 'a classic gesture of defiance'.[39] Markievicz believed that 'sending you to jail is like pulling out all the loud stops on all the speeches you ever made or words you ever wrote!' and was, for her, 'the best thing that could have happened for Ireland' because 'there was so little to be done there, only propaganda'.[40] While Markievicz maintained high spirits during her imprisonment, Gonne suffered acutely, both physically and emotionally. The pain expressed in Oscar Wilde's *De Profundis*, a poem she later acquired, would have resonated with her during her time in Holloway, when she learned of the death of her sister Kathleen and of her former lover, Millevoye.[41] Her health declined rapidly during her imprisonment and she was transferred to a sanatorium in November 1918. The Chief Secretary signed an order directing that Gonne should remain within a radius of five miles of the sanatorium until further order.[42] Nonetheless, on 23 November, Gonne managed to make a dramatic escape from the sanatorium. Disguised as a nurse, she set out to London to board the Irish mail boat that would transfer her safely back to Dublin. Iseult stayed with Ezra Pound during Gonne's imprisonment, forming a relationship with Francis Stuart, a writer known to Pound and Yeats, who was eight years her junior. Following her escape from England, it was decided that Gonne would be left in peace to reside in Dublin, even though Ezra Pound noted that she would not give any assurance of good behaviour.[43] The police were instructed to keep Gonne's movements under observation and to alert the office of the Chief Secretary if she was seen to be 'taking part in politics or in any way acting in a manner which would be prejudicial to the public safety'.[44]

Gonne's imprisonment was ultimately useful for her politically in relation to her work for amnesty associations. She wrote that her own arrest was 'typical of hundreds of the arrests now taking place'.[45] Free State officers were raiding houses and arresting individuals without a warrant. Gonne noted, 'the prisoner is then lodged in jail in secret, no communication with the outside world permitted, no solicitor allowed in, no redress possible.'[46] In her letter to the *Daily Express* in which she publicised the nature of arrests, she stated that she was 'grateful to the ignorant young ape of a Free State officer' for giving her the opportunity to report on conditions in Mountjoy Prison.[47] First-hand experience bolstered her continuing campaign to secure special rights for political prisoners. This was an ongoing concern for Gonne, but one that shifted from a British to an Irish context in the aftermath of the Treaty with the British government.

CHAPTER EIGHT

The Treaty and After

On 24 June 1921 David Lloyd George wrote to Éamon de Valera inviting him to a meeting 'to end the ruinous conflict which has for centuries divided Ireland'.[1] The following autumn, five Irish delegates set out for London to begin the peace negotiations that resulted in the Treaty, which created an Irish Free State within the British Empire for 26 counties of Ireland. The Treaty drove a division between Gonne, who initially supported the Free State position, and her son, Seán, who supported the republican side.[2] When Seán and a group of soldiers sought to establish a republican government taking hold of the Four Courts, and four men were shot there during the shelling, Gonne changed allegiance.[3] Distressed by the Civil War that erupted after the shelling of the Four Courts, she brought together a delegation of women to try to reconcile the Free State and republican sides and to halt the fighting at least until the Dáil could meet and perhaps find a way of restoring unity to the national cause. The Women's Peace Committee had two delegations, each assigned to one side of the conflict to ask for cessation of hostilities and to ask that the question of the Civil War be decided by the people. When Gonne asked Griffith as leader of the Free State government for a ceasefire, he refused, insisting that republicans surrender their arms. Gonne thus concluded that 'the whole blame of the civil war will rest on the Free State ministers.'[4] A friendship of 20 years ended, Gonne later lamenting that 'if

Willie Rooney had lived, his influence may have prevented Griffith accepting the disastrous Treaty of 1922.'[5] Ultimately, she claimed that she refused to take sides in a war that had been 'engineered by England immediately after the truce through her instrument the Orange Institution'.[6]

Gonne formed a significant new friendship in the 1920s with Charlotte Despard, the sister of Lord French, a British government official in Dublin, widow of a colonel in the Indian Army and Irish republican. She was a natural ally for Gonne and together, in the wake of the Treaty, they campaigned for the release of political prisoners through public demonstrations, letters and publications. In one such letter addressed 'To Irishmen and Women', Gonne and Despard charged General Mulcahy and members of the Free State government with knowledge and concealment of the torture of untried prisoners in Ireland for the purposes of extracting information.[7]

Their activities on behalf of prisoners resulted in their own imprisonment. Cosgrave's Coercion Act of 1923 announced that those engaged in any act of war, including anti-government proclamations, faced death if captured. As the activities of the Women's Prisoners' Defence League fell under this Act, Gonne was arrested on 10 April and sent to Kilmainham under the charges of painting banners for seditious demonstrations and preparing anti-government literature. She immediately went on hunger strike and was released after 20 days, when, after losing 16lbs, she was carried out on a stretcher in front of crowds of her supporters.[8] Although she was probably released due to fears about her potential martyrdom if she died in prison, Gonne attributed her release, in part, to Despard's influence on the press.[9] On her release she continued to campaign for prisoners, pointing out that there were more political prisoners than ever in Ireland under the Free State government.[10] She worked relentlessly for prisoners in many ways, coming up with an escape plan for six Sinn Féin prisoners in Strangeway Gaol and financially supporting families of republican prisoners in the wake of the Treaty.[11] In 1922, Gonne moved from her St Stephen's Green residence into Roebuck House, owned by Despard, where they were visited by 'exclusively political people'.[12]

Under the direction of Gonne and Despard, Roebuck House became a centre for IRA activity after the Treaty, under cover of more legitimate activities such as the jam factory they ran there.[13] The profits of the jam factory barely covered the cost of wages, which were minimal, although those who worked there were grateful for the employment.[14] Money to support unemployed republicans, which was forthcoming primarily from America, funded the rebuilding of factories and the feeding of children.[15] Seán MacBride resided in Roebuck House. Iseult had eloped to England with Francis Stuart whom she married in 1920 after encouragement from Gonne to help salvage her daughter's reputation. Although the marriage soon foundered, Stuart remained linked with IRA circles. He was interned for gun running and on his release in 1923 he spent six months at Roebuck House, which he described as a 'sort of barracks' that was used 'not so much [for] training as [for] lectures on arms and the use of arms'.[16] Arms were recovered from a van containing Gonne's furniture in 1920 and Roebuck House was ultimately ransacked during the Civil War, when the republican files of Black and Tan atrocities Gonne had held were burnt in an enormous bonfire in a Free State raid.[17]

While facilitating IRA activity, Gonne and Despard spent their time involved in what Karen Steele describes as 'street theatre'.[18] They formed 'The Mothers', a group of women who met weekly on Sundays at the ruins by the GPO on O'Connell Street and recited the rosary outside Mountjoy Prison 'in the hopes that the hearts of the English might be melted.'[19] Sheila Humphreys records that:

Madame would prepare her speech with the same care as if she was giving it to Congress [. . .] Mrs Despard and others would take part too, but often, often it was Madame on her own. She never missed a week.[20]

While remaining committed to propaganda activities within the public sphere, Gonne was also recruited for a more formal role in the Irish publicity campaign for those who suffered most during the Civil War. Under direction from Desmond Fitzgerald who, with Erskine Childers, held the role of Director of the Dáil Department of Propaganda from 1919 to 1921, Gonne apprised visitors of the reality of Ireland's situation.[21] On returning from Dublin, one journalist was told the itinerary had been carefully stage managed by the propaganda department:

You went to Kilteragh, the home of Sir Horace Plunkett, and you had a couple of hours with George Russell at Plunkett House. Desmond Fitzgerald called on you at the Shelbourne Hotel, and with an elaborate show of secrecy arranged an interview with Arthur Griffith. One or two harmless young Catholic priests fell into conversation with you at the Shelbourne. You had invitations to tea from Mrs Erskine Childers, Maud Gonne MacBride and Mrs Stopford Green, who described the atrocities they claim to have seen . . .[22]

Gonne's activities were monitored by Dublin Castle, who referred to this carefully arranged itinerary of organised propaganda and rehearsed conversations as the 'republican scenic railway'.[23]

In 1932, Yeats, recently appointed Senator by the Free State government, described Gonne as protesting 'in sybilline age, as once in youth and beauty, against what seems to her a tyranny'.[24] These few words, loaded with cynicism for the cause and with the perspective of a wistful former suitor, echo more general attitudes toward Gonne and her cause from the 1920s. Perhaps on account of widespread political exhaustion in the aftermath of the Civil War, and partly on account of her waning power to fascinate a crowd, Gonne's presence seems no longer to have had the electrifying effect that many had attested to in the days of *Cathleen*. Some thought her wearing of a long black flowing veil and posturing as 'the Eternal Widow' was 'a bit much'.[25] Gonne and Despard became known as 'Maude gone mad and Mrs Desperate'.[26] They were described variously as 'hair-beaters' (a hair beater, being 'the one that's always making a row') and 'notice-boxes'.[27] To many people the particular activities they engaged in seemed juvenile. Tony Woods, who occupied the Four Courts during the Civil War, described how the governor of Mountjoy used to tell him: 'Your mother is outside with [. . .] Maud Gonne and Miss Desparet . . . and they used to come outside the jail, shouting up to us, asking us were we all killed + shot', which, to Woods's mind, was 'futile propaganda'.[28] Kit MacBride likewise commented: 'I didn't like her type of propaganda, her exaggeration. We did have arguments about it.'[29] Her son-in-law, Francis Stuart, wrote of her activities at this time, noting 'She always gave me the impression of extraordinary activity, ceaseless activity.'[30] He recalled that 'she did write a lot and spoke a lot. I should imagine her value would have been abroad, possibly in America and possibly say in France, but how far that was valuable, really, I don't know.'[31] But he did not doubt the value of her practical support, his impression being that her impact at this time was 'far more on the side of helping [. . .] the families of prisoners'.[32]

While Ethel Mannin criticised Gonne for playing up her role as the 'Eternal Widow', Máire Comerford attests to the importance of the 'Easter Widows' for their propaganda but also for their provision of practical aid. 'Praying for the dead and collecting money for the support of the living dependents of men killed or in prison', she wrote,' 'were the first concern of those republicans who were at liberty after the Rising. In this work the widows of the executed leaders were the rallying point.'[33]

At the height of the Land War, the Ladies' Land League ensured that the families of prisoners were supported financially. Continuing this work, drawing on her exceptional skill in administering aid and drawing on her American contacts, Gonne took a central role. At Griffith's request, she established a White Cross to distribute funds acquired by the American Committee for the Relief of Ireland in 1921.[34] The following year Gonne and Despard formed the Women's Prisoners' Defence League which established the Irish Republican Prisoners Dependents' Fund, and they appointed John R. Reynolds to oversee the fund out of offices in College Street.[35] One year after the Rising it was calculated that £107,069 had been collected during the year.[36] In 1923, the fund enabled the Defence League to open a convalescent home in Harcourt Street for prisoners released on account of hunger strike. The fund was also a political tool, becoming a significant element in the development of a republican network after the Treaty. When Collins became secretary of the fund, he had the opportunity to prove his talent for organisation, and his gift for attracting and leading men.[37] Also, as Comerford notes, the relief funds distributed supported organisers of the IRB, Volunteers and Sinn Féin 'and in this way contributed to the quick re-organisation after the Rising'.[38] Gonne and Despard continued to play a key role in supporting prisoners and their families throughout the 1930s, providing employment for unemployed republicans. In 1931, when the National Aid Association formed to support republicans forced out of employment, Gonne was made chair and Hanna Sheehy-Skeffington and Charlotte Despard were made treasurers.

One of Gonne's primary post-Treaty concerns was to publicise the living conditions of Catholics in the six counties that remained under direct British rule.[39] In June 1922 Gonne accepted a mission under Desmond Fitzgerald, then Minister of Publicity for the Provisional Government, to go to Paris to write up in the Press and make known abroad 'the fiendish murder of Catholics, especially Catholic children, which was being carried on by the Orangemen and Freemasons of Belfast.'[40] Gonne was supplied with documents for this role by a special bureau established by the provisional government. Located in the basement of government buildings, Merrion Street, its chief work was 'to collect and classify Orange crimes'.[41] In 'An Appeal to our Race', Gonne outlined the nature of the persecution of Catholics in the North: 'This persecution ranges from economic pressure driving Catholics from their employment, starving and penalising their schools, depriving them of fair representation on all public bodies, to the naked horror of pogroms, shooting of old people and children in the streets of Belfast, burning and looting their houses, wrecking their churches, desecrating their graveyards, and bombing their meeting halls.'[42] The arrival of Catholic refugees from the North was another source of tension between Gonne and Griffith who, she records, said 'The IRA have no right to bring down refugees from the North; it is not our policy and we are the government,' to which she replied 'The I.R.A. have not brought the refugees [. . .]. The refugees have come themselves. They remind me of the piteous refugees from the war areas I saw round the Gare St. Lazare in Paris in 1914, and the French Government did not leave them on the streets, but allotted public buildings to the relief committees to house them.'[43] She requested Griffith, as head of the provisional government, to ask for beds. Griffith replied: 'until we show we have established order here we can't expect the plebiscite in the North Lloyd George has promised, and we want that plebescite as soon as possible for it will stop Partition.'[44] Eventually the provisional government opened a place to house the refugees, but until then Gonne invested her energies into rehousing Catholic evacuees from the pogroms in the North and inaugurating a Central Relief fund to fund practical aid.[45]

In 1937, in response to Article 2a of the Coercion Act – in which the Free State warned the entire press against publishing news of prisoners – Gonne established *Prison Bars*, a monthly newssheet devoted to listing names of those imprisoned for political reasons and pointing out violations of their rights. When the Coercion Act was abolished and the men imprisoned under it were released, the Women's Prisoners' Defence League decided to keep publishing *Prison Bars* until the anti-partition movement was strong enough to ensure publicity for the 'horrible conditions prevailing in the 6-counties under the Union Jack.'[46] *Prison Bars* remained 'the only paper writing seriously for the north', raising awareness of the ongoing persecution of Catholics that Gonne witnessed first hand.[47]

Gonne appealed for subscriptions for the National Anti-Partition Council to hold public meetings in every Irish county and to circulate literature showing the disastrous consequences of partition, highlighting that Catholics were paying the major portion of rents in the six counties but were unable to get jobs.[48] She argued that a judicial court should make awards to those victimised in the North, 'so that when partition ended they would be paid what was due to them'.[49] Conscious that England was spending a lot on propaganda in America, Gonne ensured that *Prison Bars* was distributed in America. She stated that she intended to use 'the last strength in [her] to work against partition'. So she wrote to Joseph McGarrity seeking to raise awareness of conditions in the six counties among Irish-Americans, and saying she wanted the American readership of *Prison Bars* to 'hustle a little.'[50] De Valera opposed partition in a forceful unscheduled speech to the League of Nations in Geneva in 1937. Subsequently, however Gonne criticised his failure to resign from the League when the question of partition was not addressed, as she believed that such an action of protest would have secured world-wide publicity.[51] She also charged de Valera with tolerating the persecution of Catholics in the North, asking for a parliamentary committee of inquiry into the actions and workings of the Orange institutions.[52] She also rejected the terms of de Valera's constitution when it was passed by a statewide plebescite in July 1937. Through the pages of *Prison Bars*, the Women's Prisoners' Defence League decried the patriarchal limitations imposed by Article 41: 'Never before have women been so united as now,' it stated, 'when they are faced with fascist proposals endangering their livelihood, cutting away their rights as human beings.'[53] Gonne stressed her point through the pseudonym under which she edited *Prison Bars*: 'a woman of no importance.'

In 1943, Gonne lamented 'The Irish race has well-spread newspaper connections all over the world [. . .] why is no effort made to enlist the help of Irish journalists? [. . .] We have the Radio but Radio Éireann is silent on the subject.'[54] Throughout the 1930s and 1940s Gonne sought to use new forms of media to address her political concerns, particularly her campaign against partition. In response to the terms of the constitution and the limited number of women represented in parliament, she particularly sought to galvanise women into political action. In an interview with Radio Éireann in June 1937, she said: 'Irish girls today there is so much work to do, we have our Republic and we have to make it as great as the dream of the men who gave our [*sic*] lives for it.'[55] She urged them to remember that 'The Irish race cannot allow their most sacred shrine to be cut off from them by an unnatural border.'[56] When the Republic of Ireland Act (1848) came into force in April 1949, conclusively ending Ireland's status as a British dominion, Gonne's final interview stressed the achievements of Inghinidhe na hÉireann, which she emphasised, were all the more remarkable in the context of 'Irish anti-feminism' at the turn of the twentieth century.[57]

Conclusion

After de Valera came to power Gonne was no longer a public figure protesting in Dublin city centre, but, in her own words: a 'prisoner of old age, waiting for release.'[1] After having spent time in a nursing home due to poor health, Charlotte Despard purchased a house in Eccles Street in Dublin, but ultimately relocated to Belfast to work there and thus Gonne's alliance with the left-leaning Despard came to an end. Despite this, and her failing health that confined her to Roebuck House, she continued to write on the rights of prisoners and to publicise the conditions of Catholics suffering from partition.[2] Living off the Gonne trust money, she remained at Roebuck House, often receiving communist nationalists as visitors.[3] She maintained a close watch on international politics, always with an interest in how they affected Ireland. She thought that communism was 'the apotheosis of Christ's teaching of the brotherhood of man and the upraising of humanity' and that the Nazi movement might have repercussions that would be favourable for Irish republicanism.[4] This was, Francis Stuart believed, not a sign of cruelty, but merely on account of having a tendency to lean toward 'fanaticism'.[5]

In her final years, Gonne was surrounded by her children and grandchildren, and also maintained close relationships with Ethel Mannin and Eileen O'Brien, occasionally receiving visitors including Monk Gibbon, the 'Grand Old Man of Irish Letters', and actor and author Micheál Mac Liammóir. Her friendship with Yeats had also ended when he accepted the honorary role of senator awarded to him by the Free State government, which voted for Flogging Acts in dealing with young republican soldiers, Gonne recalled, 'That was too much for me.'[6] He had also tactlessly sought to meet her at the Ascendancy club for what was to be one of their last meetings.[7] Nonetheless, in *Scattering Branches: Tributes to the Memory of W. B. Yeats* (1940), she paid tribute to the 'great work' he did for Ireland through the Literary Revival, without which she doubted there would have been the 'glorification of beauty and heroic virtue' of Easter week.[8] She had always valued Yeats as a writer and had written to him in 1915, thanking him for the many poems he had written for her. Ironically, given posterity's treatment of her, she tentatively suggested: 'Perhaps when we are dead I shall be known by those poems of yours—'[9]

In her final years, Gonne longed for the release of death. She died of cardiac failure aged 86 at Roebuck House on 27 April 1953. Two days later she was honoured with a state funeral. Behind her children and grandchildren, veterans from Inghinidhe na hÉireann, Cumann na mBan and the IRA processed to her place of rest in the Republican Plot in Glasnevin Cemetery. The O'Rahilly, a family friend, gave the funeral oration. On 1 May, the *Derry Journal* gave an overview of her life, commending her great commitment to evicted tenants and prisoners. 'The great tribute that Dublin paid on Wednesday at the funeral at the Republican Plot of Madame Maud Gonne MacBride,' it reported, 'was an expression not only of the nation's sorrow at her death but of the affection in which she was held in every part of the land. Ireland and the Irish people owe much to her, and none more than the peasant farmers of Donegal whose battles she fought with such tenacious courage against a merciless landlordism.'[10] Although laudatory, this tribute is typical in its focus on Gonne's early years and does not do full justice to her tireless campaigning for justice throughout her life in her international campaign for social and political justice for the most marginalised figures in Ireland and abroad.

In *A Servant of the Queen*, Gonne writes: 'Everyone must work according to his temperament. It was my philosophy applied to art and politics. I never willingly discouraged either a Dynamiter or a constitutionalist, a realist or a lyrical writer. My chief preoccupation was how their work could help forward the Irish Separatist movement.'[11] She refers to herself as 'one-idea'd', that idea being separatism, without that clearly meaning either Home Rule or full political independence. While she valued the focus she had through following the principle that 'the enemy of my enemy is my friend', others viewed the danger of her 'fanaticism' that could lead her to align her views with Boulangists, Bolsheviks and communists, irrespective of the implications of their political ideals beyond how they might support the Irish separatist movement.[12] Yet, one of Gonne's chief strengths was her refusal to commit to any specific element of the nationalist movement and her ability to speak for the cause rather than the faction. Although spellbound by Gonne, Yeats was able to rationalise her power over crowds 'even when pushing an abstract principle to what seemed [. . .] an absurdity'. He saw this power as a consequence of her beauty that 'moved minds full of old Gaelic stories and poems' because she seemed to belong to an ancient civilisation; her beauty itself 'suggested joy and freedom'.[13] In her visionary opening of *A Servant of the Queen*, Gonne merges the image of a mystical Queen, Cathleen ni Houlihan, with her own belief, 'that courage and will are unconquerable and, where allied to the mysterious forces of the land, can accomplish anything.'[14]

The symbolic power that Yeats harnessed in the role of Cathleen ni Houlihan, and that Gonne attributed to the power of the land working through her as one of the 'stones' on which the Queen rested, was to have a diffuse and enduring effect. It consolidated the power and political agency of Inghinidhe na hÉireann and represented an ideal to be fought for through years to come. The power of Gonne's 'Queen' symbolism in drama and in her memoir is reflected not only in the words of her contemporaries but through the literature of the next generation. In a journal kept while on hunger strike, Frank Gallagher wrote of his faith in the struggle for independence: 'If we fail, the nation fails . . . if we succeed, Ireland becomes more than ever "the young girl with the walk of a Queen"'.[15]

Notes

Introduction

1   The Under-Secretary of the Lord-Lieutenant in Dublin refuted this claim. See 'An Irish martyr', in *The National Observer* 7:166 (23 Jan. 1892), pp 246–7.

2   Maud Gonne, *The Autobiography of Maud Gonne: A Servant of the Queen* (Chicago, 1995), p. 152.

3   'Ireland and Irish-America', *United Irishman* (22 June 1901), reprinted in Karen Steele (ed.), *Maud Gonne's Irish Nationalist Writings* (Dublin, 2004), p. 182.

4   Maud Gonne MacBride interview, no date, with notes by Conrad Balliet and photocopy of published interview. Maud Gonne Collection Series 2: Interviews, 1937.

5   Philip H. Bagenal, *The American Irish and their Influence on Irish Politics* (London, 1882), p. 129.

6   'Ireland and Irish-America', p. 183.

7   Máire Comerford papers, University College Dublin Archives, LA18/12(1).

8   Interview with Maud Gonne MacBride by DrD [Leslie de Barra?] *c.* 1950, p. 5. National Library of Ireland Manuscript (hereafter, NLI MS) 35,976.

9   Likewise, Barry Shortall's *Willie and Maud: A Love Story* (2002) and Margery Brady's *Love Story of Yeats and Maud Gonne* (2012) remain, as their titles suggest, entranced by Yeats's unrequited love.

10   Interview with Kit MacBride, 9 July 1974. Research Files of Conrad Balliet. Series 2 Interviews, 1937, 1973–8. Box 1: Folders 18–41, AV1, p. 1.

11   W. T. Stead, 'The progress of the world', in *The Review of Reviews* 5: 25 (Jan. 1892), p. 4.

12   Gonne, *A Servant of the Queen*, p. 164.

Chapter 1

1   *Surrey and Hants News, Farnham Advertiser, Guildford Times, Aldershot Gazette,* Saturday 29 Dec. 1966. Research files of Conrad Balliet. Series 3 Research files of Conrad Balliet, Box 2–Box 5: Folder 5; OP1.

2   Ibid., 'Burial Record of infant sister of Maud Gonne', 1872.

3   Maud Gonne, *The Autobiography of Maud Gonne: A Servant of the Queen* (Chicago, 1995), p. 11.

4   Ibid., p. 17.

5   Maud Gonne MacBride, Witness statement for the Bureau of Military History (hereafter, BMH WS), available at http://www.bureauofmilitaryhistory. ie/reels/bmh/BMH.WS0317.pdf; Gonne, *A Servant of the Queen*, p. 166, 173.

6   Gonne, *A Servant of the Queen*, p. 25. Seán MacBride attributed her political and social concerns to the influence of the nurse she had in Howth. Conrad Balliet interview notes, p. 9.

7   Notes from an interview with Thora Forrester. Conrad Balliet Research Notes, p. 114.

8   Letter from Thomas Gonne to Maud Gonne on (11 July [year not given]). Research Files of Conrad Balliet. Series 1 Correspondence, *c.* 1902–50. Box 1: Folders 1–17.

9   Letter from Thomas Gonne to Maud Gonne on (20 Dec. [year not given]), in ibid.

10   Letter from Thomas Gonne to Maud Gonne and Kathleen Gonne (26 June, 1880), in ibid.

11   Gonne, *A Servant of the Queen*, p. 11, pp 15–16.

12   Seán MacBride, Conrad Balliet interview notes, 16 July 1973, p. 1. Series 2 Interviews, 1937, 1973–8 Box 1: Folders 18–41, AV1.

13   Interview with Kit MacBride, 9 July 1974. Research Files of Conrad Balliet. Series 2 Interviews, 1937, 1973–8. Box 1: Folders 18–41, AV1, p. 1.

14   Maud Gonne MacBride, BMH WS.

15   Maud Gonne to Ethel Mannin, 3 May 1945, National Library of Ireland (hereafter, NLI).

16   Gonne, *A Servant of the Queen*, p. 42.

17   Transcript of untitled radio broadcast by Maud Gonne, May 1937, Series 2 Interviews, 1937, 1973–8 Box 1: Folders 18–41, AV1, p. 24.

18   Gonne, *A Servant of the Queen*, p. 48.

19   Eileen is referred to as 'Daphne' in ibid., pp 53–5.

20   Ibid., p. 59.

21 Imogen Stuart interview transcript, 11 July 1973. Series 2 Interviews, 1937, 1973–8 Box 1: Folders 18–41, AV1.

22 Gonne, *A Servant of the Queen*, p. 60.

23 Francis Stuart interview transcript, 4 July 1973. Series 2 Interviews, 1937, 1973–8 Box 1: Folders 18–41, AV1.

24 Gonne, *A Servant of the Queen*, p. 62.

25 Maud (Edith) Gonne entry, Deirdre Toomey, *Oxford Dictionary of Irish Biography* (Oxford, 2008).

26 Gonne, *A Servant of the Queen*, p. 65.

27 Ibid., pp 67–76.

28 Adrian N. Mulligan, '"By a thousand ingenious devices": The Ladies' Land League and the development of Irish nationalism', in *Historical Geography* 37 (2009), p. 172.

29 Gonne, *A Servant of the Queen*, pp 78–9.

30 Ibid., p. 79.

Chapter 2

1 Maud Gonne, *The Autobiography of Maud Gonne: A Servant of the Queen* (Chicago, 1995), p. 93.

2 Ibid.

3 Interview with Maud Gonne MacBride by DrD [Leslie de Barra?] *c.* 1950, p. 7. National Library of Ireland Manuscript (hereafter, NLI MS) 35,976.

4 Maud Gonne, 'The value of debating societies', in NLI.

5 Gonne, *A Servant of the Queen*, p. 99.

6 Ibid., p. 98.

7 Mary L. Macken, 'Yeats, O'Leary and the Contemporary Club', in *Studies: An Irish Quarterly Review* 28:109 (1939), p. 139.

8 Gonne, *A Servant of the Queen*, p. 98.

9 Ibid., p. 99.

10 Ibid., p. 100.

11 Ibid., p. 102.

12 William Ready, Superintendent of the Dublin Military Police, sent a long report on M. G. to his superior, Major Cosselin. DSP, cbs 1833/8 cited by Conrad Balliet, '"Maud Gonne: A documented chronology", Drafts'. Series 3 Research files of Conrad Balliet Box 2–Box 5: Folder 5; OP1.

13 'Patriotic Children's Treat', in *United Irishman* (5 May 1900), p. 8.

14 Gonne, *A Servant of the Queen*, p. 116.

15 Ibid., p. 138. I can find no support for the claim that she was given this appellation in contemporary accounts of Gonne's activity during the evictions.

16 Letter from Londonderry, Ireland, 'Afoot in Ireland', in *Morning Journal and Courier* (27 July 1889), p. 1.

17 Seán MacBride, interview transcript, 16 July 1973. Conrad Balliet Research Files, Series 2 Interviews, 1937, 1973–8 Box 1: Folders 18–41, AV1; Letter from Thora Forrester to Conrad Balliet, 4 Aug. 1973. Research Files of Conrad Balliet. Series 1 Correspondence, *c.* 1902–50 Box 1: Folders 1–17.

18 Gonne, *A Servant of the Queen*, p. 135.

19 Ibid., p. 143.

20 Ibid.

21 Ibid.

22 Ibid., p. 121.

23 Ibid., p. 162.

24 Transcript of untitled radio broadcast by Maud Gonne, May 1937, p. 27. Research Files of Conrad Balliet. Series 2 Interviews, 1937, 1973–8 Box 1: Folders 18–41, AV1; *Freeman's Journal*, 6 Apr. 1892.

25 Transcript of untitled radio broadcast by Maud Gonne, May 1937, p. 26.

26 Senia Pašeta, '1798 in 1898: The politics of commemoration', in *Irish Review*, 22 (1998), p. 50.

27 Donall O Luanaigh, 'Fenianism and France in March 1867: Some comments on the Irish insurrection', in *Études Irlandaises* 15:2 (1990), p. 107.

28 Denis Donoghue (ed. and trans.), W. B. Yeats, *Memoirs* (London, 1972), p. 41.

29 Ibid.

30 Gonne, *A Servant of the Queen*, p. 161.

31 Yeats, *Memoirs*, p. 46.

32 Ibid., p. 133.

33 Letter from W. B. Yeats to George Russell [1 Nov. 1891], in John Kelly (ed.), *The Collected Letters of W. B. Yeats*, Volume 1, 1865–1895 (Oxford, 1986), p. 266.

34 Anna MacBride White and A. Norman Jeffares (eds), *The Gonne-Yeats Letters 1893–1938: Always Your Friend* (London, 1992), p. 81.

35 Maud Gonne MacBride interview, no date, with notes by Conrad Balliet, p. 3. Research Files of Conrad Balliet. Series 2 Interviews, 1937, 1973–8 Box 1: Folders 18–41, AV1.

36 *Gonne-Yeats Letters 1893–1938*, p. 108.

37 Ibid., p. 128.

38 Gonne, *A Servant of the Queen*, p. 161.

39 Ibid.

Chapter 3

1   'Royal Com. To Inquire into Working of Penal Servitude Acts. Report, Minutes of Evidence, Appendix, Index', in House of Commons Parliamentary Papers, 1878–9, Command Papers.

2   See Michael Davitt, 'The treatment of political prisoners', in *The Pall Mall Gazette*, 7476, (4 Mar. 1889).

3   Gonne's account of a visit to Portland Prison in *The Servant of the Queen* makes unsubstantiated claims that she secured the early release of a number of prisoners, as she said she had promised she would when she met them and entered into a trance-like state. Conrad Balliet followed up on the case of George Gilmore, who was sentenced to 18 months in Mountjoy Prison in 1927 for his political activities and he served the full term. Gilmore stated to Balliet that he was only released when de Valera came to power in 1932. See Research Files of Conrad Balliet, p. 103. Nonetheless, for her tireless efforts for political prisoners, Gonne was granted the freedom of the city of Limerick in 1900.

4   Maud Gonne, *The Autobiography of Maud Gonne: A Servant of the Queen* (Chicago, 1995), p. 96.

5   Christy Campbell, *Fenian Fire: The British Government Plot to Assassinate Queen Victoria* (London, 2002), p. 310n.

6   Michael Davitt, *Leaves from a Prison Diary; or, Lectures to a 'Solitary' Audience*, vol. 2 (London, 1885), pp 160–1.

7   Gonne, *A Servant of the Queen*, p. 132.

8   Ibid., p. 138.

9   'Evictions in Donegal', House of Commons debate (11 Apr. 1889) vol 335   cc 219–21.

10   Transcript of untitled radio broadcast by Maud Gonne, May 1937, Series 2 Interviews, 1937, 1973–8 Box 1: Folders 18–41, AV1, p. 25.

11   Chris Healy, *Confessions of a Journalist* (London, 1904), p. 228.

12   Ibid.

13   Charles Gavan Duffy, *Four Years of Irish History: 1845–1849* (London and New York, 1883), p. 448n.

14   Eleanor Fitzsimons, *Wilde's Women: How Oscar Wilde was Shaped by the Women He Knew* (London, 2016), p. 27.

15   W. B. Yeats, 'The New Speranza', supplement of *La Revue Catholique*, reprinted in *United Ireland* (16 Jan. 1892). Reprinted as 'Maude Gonne' in Horace Reynolds (ed.), *Letters to the New Island* (Oxford, 1970), p. 151.

16   Ibid.

17   Karen Steele, 'Raising her voice for justice: Maud Gonne and the *United Irishman*', in *New Hibernia Review / Iris Éireannach Nua* 3:2 (1999), p. 88.

18 Yeats, 'Maude Gonne', pp 152–3.

19 Ibid., p. 153.

20 Denis Donoghue (ed. and trans.), W. B. Yeats, *Memoirs* (London, 1972), p. 41.

21 Interview with Maud Gonne MacBride by D. D [Leslie de Barra?] c. 1950, p. 4. National Library of Ireland Manuscript (hereafter, NLI MS) 35,976.

22 Gonne, *A Servant of the Queen*, p. 148.

23 C. L. Innes, 'A voice in directing the affairs of Ireland': *L'Irlande Libre*, *The Shan Van Vocht* and *Bean na h-Éireann*', in Paul Hyland and Neil Sammells (eds), *Irish Writing: Exile and Subversion* (London, 1991), p. 148.

24 Ibid., p. 150.

25 'Dans ce titre, expression, de notre espérance, nous plaçons tout le programme de nos revendications nationales; est c'est à la France, pays si cher aux opprimés, que nous venons jeter ce cri de liberté. D'ailleurs ne sommes nous pas Caltes aussi, fils de la même race, et notre sang n'a-t-il pas coulé maintes fois sur les mêmes champs de batailles, sous nos drapeaux alliés?', quoted in ibid, p. 149. Translation by Sean Ferguson.

26 Healy, *Confessions of a Journalist*, p. 228.

27 Gonne estimated that she received around 2,000 cuttings from the French press following her tour. Gonne, *A Servant of the Queen*, p. 162; W. T. Stead, 'The progress of the world', in *The Review of Reviews* 5:25 (Jan. 1892), p. 4.

28 Gonne, *A Servant of the Queen*, p. 170.

29 Ibid., p. 171.

30 *Freeman's Journal*, (6 Apr. 1892).

31 Ibid., (16 June 1892).

32 Ibid.

33 Ibid.

34 Maud Gonne, 'Branding', published in *Republic of Ireland* in 1922, reprinted in Karen Steele (ed.), *Maud Gonne's Irish Nationalist Writings* (Dublin, 2004), p. 26.

35 'Those who are suffering for Ireland', in *Northern Patriot* (29 Nov. 1895), in ibid., pp 6–7.

36 Gonne, *A Servant of the Queen*, p. 183.

37 Ibid., pp 178–9.

38 Ibid., p. 187.

39 Gonne later transcribed figures from Mulhall's *Fifty Years of National Progress* in a series of short documents of statistics entitled 'Ireland under Victoria 1837–1900' published in *L'Irlande Libre* and in *United Irishman* in May 1900.

40 'Anti-Jubilee demonstration in Dublin', *Freeman's Journal* (22 June 1897), p. 6.

41 'Maud Gonne here', in *Irish-American Weekly* (16 Feb. 1901).

42 'Sons of Erin find little cause for rejoicing at the Jubilee', in *The Topeka State Journal* (22 June 1897).

43 'Fiery speech', in *The Daily Ardmoreite* (30 June 1897).

44 'For the honour of the Queen', *Pall Mall Gazette* (6 Dec. 1899).

45 PRO 903 8, cited by Conrad Balliet, 'For the love of Maud', p. 130. Series 3 Research files of Conrad Balliet Box 2–Box 5: Folder 5; OP1.

Chapter 4

1 W. B. Yeats, 'Maude Gonne', in Horace Reynolds (ed.), *Letters to the New Island* (Oxford, 1970), p. 150.

2 Anna MacBride White and A. Norman Jeffares (eds), *The Gonne-Yeats Letters 1893–1938: Always Your Friend* (London, 1992), p. 468n.

3 Maud Gonne, *The Autobiography of Maud Gonne: A Servant of the Queen* (Chicago, 1995), p. 222.

4 *The Irish Standard* (27 Nov. 1897).

5 See Conrad Balliet, 'For the love of Maud' in research notes on Maud Gonne's trips to the United States. Series 3 Research Files of Conrad Balliet, Box2–Box5: Folder 5; OP1.

6 Parnell, for example was reported as speaking 'without "magnetism" ... without a single characteristic to be expected of a noted Irish agitator.' 'Editor's easy chair', *Harper's Monthly* 40 (March 1880), p. 627.

7 *New York Times* (25 Oct. 1897).

8 'Miss Maud Gonne, the Irish heroine, on Ireland's woes', in the *San Francisco Call* (7 Nov. 1897).

9 *The Irish Standard* (30 Oct. 1897).

10 See, for example, 'An Irish heroine', *The Irish Times*, (15 Aug. 1896), which reprints an article on Gonne published in the *New York Herald*. Also 'Miss Maud Gonne', in *The Record-Union* (6 June 1897), and 'Miss Maud Gonne coming', in the *Irish Standard* (20 Nov. 1897).

11 According to the *San Francisco Call* (7 Nov. 1897), it is the Parisians who named her Joan of Arc.

12 Gonne, *A Servant of the Queen*, p. 90; Letter from Maud Gonne to John Quinn (20 Nov. 1913). Commending Pádraig Pearse, Gonne wrote that he is 'after my old friend J. F. Taylor, the greatest orator I have ever heard.' See Janis and Richard Londraville (eds), *Too Long a Sacrifice: The Letters of Maud Gonne and John Quinn* (Selinsgrove, 1999), p. 111.

13 'Pleading for Old Ireland', in *Omaha Daily Bee* (27 Nov. 1897).

14 'Miss Maud Gonne, the Irish heroine, on Ireland's woes', *The San Francisco Call*.

15 For details of the split in Clan na Gael, see Owen McGee, *The IRB: The Irish Republican Brotherhood from the Land League to Sinn Féin* (Dublin, 2005), pp 105–8; John Devoy, 'Story of the Clan na Gael', in *Gaelic American* (29 Nov. 1924); and Niall Whelehan, *The Dynamiters: Irish Nationalism and Political Violence in the Wider World* (Cambridge, 2012).

16 Gonne, *A Servant of the Queen*, p. 234.

17 'The Absence of Miss Gonne', in *The Irish Standard* (11 Dec. 1897).

18 C. L. Innes, 'A voice in directing the affairs of Ireland': *L'Irlande Libre*, *The Shan Van Vocht* and *Bean na h-Éireann*', in Paul Hyland and Neil Sammells (eds), *Irish Writing: Exile and Subversion* (London, 1991), p. 150.

19 'The Irish Joan of Arc', in *Topeka State Journal* (24 Nov. 1897).

20 Ibid.

21 Ibid.

22 Nelson M. Blake, 'The Olney-Pauncefote Treaty of 1897', in *The American Historical Review* 50:2 (Jan. 1945), p. 237.

23 'The Maud Gonne reception', in *Irish-American Weekly* (Jan. 1900).

24 'Ireland's "Joan of Arc"', in *The Topeka State Journal* (17 Mar. 1900), last edn.

25 'Time for Ireland to rise', in *National Labor Tribune* (1 Feb. 1900); In a letter to Lady Gregory on 29 March 1900, Yeats reported that 'Maud Gonne is seriously ill with *enteritis* and will hardly be well in time to do anything with the crowds.' See, Warwick Gould et al. (eds), *The Collected Letters of W. B. Yeats* (Oxford, 1997), p. 506.

26 Anna MacBride White and A. Norman Jeffares (eds), *The Gonne-Yeats Letters 1893–1938: Always Your Friend* (London, 1992), p. 130.

27 W. B. Yeats, 'The freedom of the press in Ireland', in *The Speaker*, reprinted in *The United Irishman* (28 July 1900), pp 7–8.

28 Letter from W. B. Yeats to John O'Leary (9 Nov. 1891), in John Kelly (ed.), *Collected Letters of W. B. Yeats. Vol 1: 1865–1895* (Oxford, 1986), p. 270.

29 Karen Steele, *Women, Press, and Politics during the Irish Revival* (Syracuse University Press, 2007), p. 68.

30 Virginia Glandon, *Arthur Griffith and the Advanced-Nationalist Press* (New York, 1985), p. 16.

31 *The Gonne-Yeats Letters 1893–1938*, p. 128.

32 *United Irishman* (20 May 1899); ibid. (27 May 1899).

33 *Shan Van Vocht*, 2(10) (Oct. 1897), cited by Senia Pašeta, *Irish Nationalist Women 1900–1918* (Cambridge, 2013), p. 19.

34 Transcript of untitled radio broadcast by Maud Gonne, May 1937, Series 2 Interviews, 1937, 1973–8 Box 1: Folders 18–41, AV1, p. 4.

Chapter 5

1 Transcript of untitled radio broadcast by Maud Gonne, May 1937, Series 2 Interviews, 1937, 1973–8 Box 1: Folders 18–41, AV1, p. 3.

2 Ibid.

3 Ibid.

4 Ibid.

5 *Bean Na hÉireann* (20 Jan. 1910), pp 3–5.

6 Transcript of untitled radio broadcast by Maud Gonne, May 1937, p. 3.

7 Ibid.

8 Ibid., p. 7.

9 'What we owe the children', in *United Irishman* (7 July 1900), p. 5.

10 Ibid.

11 Transcript of untitled radio broadcast by Maud Gonne, May 1937, p. 8.

12 Ibid., p. 7.

13 Ibid.

14 Keating, Mercedes, notes, 2 July 1973. Conrad Balliet Research Files, Series 2 Interviews, 1937, 1973–8 Box 1: Folders 18–41, AV1.

15 'Maud Gonne here', in *Irish-American Weekly* (16 Feb. 1901).

16 Witness statement for the Bureau of Military History (hereafter, BMH WS), 391: Helena Molony cited by Senia Pašeta, in *Irish Nationalist Women 1900–1918* (Cambridge, 2013), p. 43.

17 Máire O'Brolchain, 'Inghinidhe na hÉireann, Dublin', quoted in Fearghal McGarry, *Rebels: Voices from the Easter Rising* (Dublin, 2011), p. 38.

18 Editorial, *Bean na hÉireann*, 1:4 (Feb. 1909).

19 'Seizure of *The United Irishman*', 14 Apr. 1900, p. 5.

20 'The libel on Miss Gonne', *The United Irishman* (28 Apr. 1900).

21 Ibid., 20 Oct. 1900.

22 Maud Gonne, *The Autobiography of Maud Gonne: A Servant of the Queen* (Chicago, 1995), p. 248.

23 'Miss Maude Gonne's visit to Liverpool' (CO 904, Boxes 193–216). Public Records Office, London, England, CO 904/202/154–166.

24 Rumours had circulated in the press in Sept.–Oct. 1901 that Gonne was en route to South Africa (see *Globe* (15 Oct. 1901), and *Waterford Standard* (16 Oct. 1901)); reports were corrected in the *Eastern Daily Press* on 17 Oct.

25 Maud Gonne, 'Preface', Lucien Gillain, *Heures de Guerite: Poesies d'un Dragon* (Paris, 1893). Translation by Sean Ferguson.

26 Anna MacBride White and A. Norman Jeffares (eds), *The Gonne-Yeats Letters 1893 1938: Always Your Friend* (London, 1992), p. 114.

27 *Heures de Guerite: Poesies d'un Dragon.*

28 Gonne, *A Servant of the Queen*, pp 280–1.

29 Ibid., p. 279.

30 Ibid.

31 Denis Donoghue identifies the agent as Frank Hugh O'Donnell in Denis Donoghue (ed. and trans.), W. B. Yeats, *Memoirs* (London, 1972), p. 116n.

32 Owen McGee, *The IRB: The Irish Republican Brotherhood from the Land League to Sinn Féin* (Dublin, 2005), p. 283.

33 Gonne, *A Servant of the Queen*, p. 310.

34 Notebook of John MacBride, National Library of Ireland Manuscript (hereafter, NLI MS) Allan papers, 29,817.

35 Gonne, *A Servant of the Queen*, p. 271.

36 Ibid., p. 308

37 Ibid., p. 321.

38 Gonne, 'Ireland and her Foreign Relations', in *United Irishman* (22 Dec. 1900), reprinted in Karen Steele (ed.), *Maud Gonne's Irish Nationalist Writings* (Dublin, 2004), p. 179.

39 Balliet, 'For the love of Maud', p. 145.

40 'The Famine Queen', in *United Irishman* (7 Apr. 1900) reprinted in Steele, *Maud Gonne's Irish Nationalist Writings*, pp 54–6, p. 55.

41 'Seditious Press (Ireland)', House of Commons debate, (25 Nov. 1914) vol 68 cc1120–1.

42 'Maud Gonne here', in *Irish-American Weekly* (16 Feb. 1901).

43 *Blackfoot News* (27 Apr. 1901).

44 Gonne, *A Servant of the Queen*, p. 313.

45 Letter from John MacBride to Honoria MacBride, NLI MS 13,770; *United Irishman* (6 Oct. 1900), p. 4.

46 Transcript of untitled radio broadcast by Maud Gonne, May 1937, p. 8.

47 Ibid, p. 9; Maud Gonne MacBride interview, no date, with notes by Conrad Balliet, p. 1.

48 Transcript of untitled radio broadcast by Maud Gonne, May 1937, pp 8–9.

49 William H. O'Donnell and Douglas N. Archibald (eds), Yeats, *The Collected Works of W. B. Yeats Volume III: Autobiographies* (New York, 1999), p. 331.

50 Pašeta, *Irish Nationalist Women , 1900–1918*, p. 53.

51 Stephen Gwynn, 'The Irish Literary Theatre and its affinities', in *Fortnightly Review* 70 (1901), p. 1051.

52 Tanya Dean, 'Staging Hibernia: Female allegories of Ireland in *Cathleen ni Houlihan* and *Dawn*', in *Theatre History Studies* 33: *Theatres of War* (2014), pp 71–82, p. 74.

53 Gonne, *A Servant of the Queen*, p. 154. Note from May 1910, in Yeats, *Memoirs*, p. 247.

54 William H. O'Donnell and Douglas N. Archibald (eds), W. B. Yeats, *The Autobiography of William Butler Yeats* (New York, 1965), p. 82.

55 Yeats, *The Collected Works of W. B. Yeats Volume III*, p. 120.

56 W. B. Yeats, *Cathleen ni Houlihan*, in Richard Allen Cave (ed.) W. B. Yeats, *Selected Plays*, (London, 1997), p. 28.

57 'Stephen Gwynn on the effect of "Cathleen ni Houlihan"', in A. Norman Jeffares (ed.), *W. B. Yeats: The Critical Heritage* (London, 1977), p. 377.

58 Chistopher Morash, *A History of Irish Theatre 1601–2000* (Cambridge, 2009), p. 123.

59 Máire Comerford papers, University College Dublin Archives (hereafter, UCDA), LA18/5(1).

60 Ibid.

61 Ibid., LA18/5(2).

62 Maud Gonne MacBride interview, no date, with notes by Conrad Balliet, p. 2.

63 'Stephen Gwynn on the effect of "Cathleen ni Houlihan"', p. 376.

64 W. B. Yeats, 'Man and the echo', in Daniel Albright (ed.), *W. B. Yeats: The Poems* (London, 1992), p. 392; W. B. Yeats, 'No second Troy', in ibid., p. 140.

65 Máire Comerford papers, UCDA, LA18/5(1).

66 Ibid., LA18/5(10).

67 *Dawn* was never performed in public. In 1904, the year in which *Dawn* was published in *United Irishman*, Gonne was living primarily in Paris, caring for a baby and taking legal advice as she sought to divorce John MacBride.

68 See George Moore, *Hail and Farewell* (London, 1926), pp 264–5 for Moore's account of Yeats's response to *The Cross or the Guillotine*, in which Yeats was accused of heresy in writing *The Countess Cathleen*.

69 Wilde wrote a number of poems inspired by the French Revolution, including 'The year of revolutions' and 'France in '93'.

70 Gonne, *Dawn*, in *United Irishman* (29 Oct. 1904), reprinted in Karen Steele (ed.), *Maud Gonne's Irish Nationalist Writings* (Dublin, 2004), p. 210.

71 'Ireland and her foreign relations', in *United Irishman* (22 Dec. 1900), p. 4.

72 Gonne, *Dawn*, p. 214; Gonne documents the working of the famine relief system as the working of 'the famine policy of the British empire' in an article

entitled 'India', published in *United Irishman* (12 May 1900), reprinted in Steele, *Maud Gonne's Irish Nationalist Writings 1895–1946*, p. 171.

73 Gonne, *A Servant of the Queen*, p. 252.

74 Gonne, *Dawn*, p. 218.

75 Ella Young, *Flowering Dusk* (London, 1945), p. 102

76 Gonne, *Dawn*, pp 205–6.

77 Gonne, 'Famine! My experiences in Mayo', in *Daily Nation* (10 Mar. 1898), reprinted in Steele, *Maud Gonne's Irish Nationalist Writings 1895–1946*, pp 115–18.

78 *The Gonne-Yeats Letters 1893–1938*, p. 152.

79 Gonne, *A Servant of the Queen*, pp 321–2.

80 Ibid., p. 322.

81 Letter from Maud Gonne to John Quinn [undated, received 6 May 1914], in Janis and Richard Londraville (eds), *Too Long a Sacrifice: The Letters of Maud Gonne and John Quinn* (Selinsgrove, 1999), p. 141.

82 *The Gonne-Yeats Letters 1893–1938*, p. 173.

Chapter 6

1 Letter from Lady Gregory to Wilfred Blunt, cited by Nancy Cardozo, *Lucky Eyes and a High Heart: The Life of Maud Gonne* (New York, 1978) p. 89.

2 Maud Gonne and James Connolly, 'The rights of life and the rights of property', in *Workers Republic* (17 Sept. 1898) *Prison Bars* (Dec. 1937), reprinted in Karen Steele (ed.), *Maud Gonne's Irish Nationalist Writings* (Dublin, 2004), pp 112–13.

3 Interview with Eileen O'Brien, transcript, 11 July 1973. Series 2 Interviews, 1937, 1973–8 Box 1: Folders 18–41, AV1.

4 Ibid.

5 Letter from Maud Gonne to Kathleen Gonne, 1902, Research Files of Conrad Balliet. Series 1 Correspondence, *c*. 1902–50 Box 1: Folders 1–17.

6 Anna MacBride White and A. Norman Jeffares (eds), *The Gonne-Yeats Letters 1893–1938: Always Your Friend* (London, 1992), p. 166.

7 Ibid., pp 164–5.

8 Ibid., p. 330, 496.

9 Maud Gonne, *The Autobiography of Maud Gonne: A Servant of the Queen* (Chicago: 1995), p. 331.

10 Ibid., p. 333.

11 Ibid.

12 Ibid., p. 334.

13 Elizabeth Coxhead, *Daughters of Erin: Five Women of the Irish Renascence* (London, 1965), p. 57.

14 Roy Foster, *W. B. Yeats, A Life: The Apprentice Mage* (Oxford, 1997), p. 286.

15 Maud Gonne MacBride to Mme Avril [undated], National Library of Ireland Manuscript (hereafter, NLI MS), 10,714.

16 Margaret Ward, *Maud Gonne: Ireland's Joan of Arc* (London, 1990), p. 78.

17 PRO 903 8, cited by Conrad Balliet, 'For the love of Maud', p. 130. Series 3 Research files of Conrad Balliet Box 2–Box 5: Folder 5; OP1. p. 99.

18 DSP 28726/S, cited in Conrad Balliet, 'Maud Gonne: A documented chronology', Drafts. Series 3 Research files of Conrad Balliet Box 2–Box 5: Folder 5; OP1.

19 Chris Healy, *Confessions of a Journalist* (London, 1904), pp 230–1.

20 Gonne, *A Servant of the Queen*, p. 323.

21 *The Gonne-Yeats Letters 1893–1938*, p. 167.

22 Transcript of untitled radio broadcast by Maud Gonne, May 1937, p. 13.

23 Ibid., p. 14.

24 Gonne gives a detailed account in her witness statement for the Witness statement for the Bureau of Military History (hereafter, BMH WS), at http://www.bureauofmilitaryhistory.ie/reels/bmh/BMH.WS0317.pdf.

25 See Gonne's BMH WS.

26 According to Gonne the politicisation of Constance Markievicz began with her joining Inghinidhe na hÉireann, her first role being to oversee the Boys' Brigade, which evolved into Fianna Éireann under her direction. See Gonne's BMH WS.

27 Molony recorded: 'I was a young girl dreaming about Ireland when I saw and heard Maud Gonne speaking by the Custom House in Dublin one Aug. evening in 1903 . . . She electrified me and filled me with some of her own spirit.' Cited by R. M. Fox in *Rebel Irishwomen* (Dublin, 1967), p. 120.

28 Maud Gonne, 'The Irish press', in *United Irishman* (7 Feb. 1903), reprinted in Steele, *Maud Gonne's Irish Nationalist Writings 1895–1946*, pp 101–8.

29 Letter from Maud Gonne to Kathleen Gonne, 1902. Research Files of Conrad Balliet. Series 1 Correspondence, circa 1902–50 Box 1: Folders 1–17.

30 Notebook of John MacBride, NLI MS, Allan papers, MS 29,817.

31 See Anthony J. Jordan and Judith Jordan (eds), *Boer War to Easter Rising: The Writings of John MacBride* (Westport, 2012), for samples of his journalism.

32 See Gonne's BMH WS.

33 Owen McGee, *The IRB: The Irish Republican Brotherhood from the Land League to Sinn Féin* (Dublin, 2005), p. 297.

34 'Is Maud Gonne English?', in *Leeds Mercury* (27 July 1905).

35 Ibid., p. 5.

36 *The Gonne-Yeats Letters 1893–1938*, pp 184–5.

37 Ibid., p. 232.

38 Alan Himber, *The Letters of John Quinn to William Butler Yeats* (Epping, 1983), p. 6.

39 'Maud Gonne's case', in *The Irish Standard* (12 Aug. 1905).

40 Healy, *Confessions of a Journalist*, p. 229.

41 John Kelly and Ronald Schuchard (eds), *The Collected Letters of W. B. Yeats: Volume IV, 1905–1907* (Oxford, 2005), p. 515.

42 Balliet, 'For the love of Maud', p. 132.

43 *The Gonne-Yeats Letters 1893–1938*, p. 184.

44 Notebook of John MacBride, NLI MS, Allan papers, MS 29,817.

45 Ibid.

46 Senator Michael Yeats, Interview Notes, 11 July 1973, Conrad Balliet Research Files, Series 2 Interviews, 1937, 1973–8 Box 1: Folders 18–41, AV1.

47 *The Gonne-Yeats Letters 1893–1938*, p. 194.

48 Ibid., p. 232.

49 Ibid.; Gonne remained in Paris until 1917, when she returned with both Iseult and Seán.

50 Balliet, 'For the love of Maud', p. 145.

51 Letter from Maud Gonne to John Quinn (15 July 1915), in Janis and Richard Londraville (eds), *Too Long a Sacrifice: The Letters of Maud Gonne and John Quinn* (Selinsgrove, 1999), p. 147.

52 See Gonne's BMH WS.

53 *The Gonne-Yeats Letters 1893–1938*, pp 266–7.

54 Ibid., p. 86.

55 Maud Gonne, 'The children must be fed', in *Bean na hÉireann* (May 1910) reprinted in Steele, *Maud Gonne's Irish Nationalist Writings*, pp 141–3.

56 Sir Charles Cameron, 'How the Dublin poor live', in *Reminiscences of Sir Charles Cameron* (Dublin, 1912), p. 174.

57 *Celtic Wonder Tales*, retold by Ella Young, illustrated and decorated by Maud Gonne (Dublin, 1910).

58 'What we owe the children', (1900) reprinted in Steele, *Maud Gonne's Irish Nationalist Writings*, p. 132.

59 Maud Gonne to John Quinn (31 Dec. 1910), in *Too Long a Sacrifice*, p. 62.

60 Maud Gonne to John Quinn (3 Nov. 1911), in ibid., p. 88.

61 *The Gonne-Yeats Letters 1893–1938*, p. 326.

62 Ibid.

63 Ibid.

64 However, Gonne's comments on socialism were in the context of a defence of Communism, which she considered 'no contradiction to the Republican ideal'.

65 Maud Gonne to John Quinn (20 Nov. 1913), in *Too Long a Sacrifice*, p. 110. Gonne describes 'how urgent it is for us to have Home Rule', a sentiment repeated in a letter of 16 Dec. 1913, in *Too Long a Sacrifice*, p. 113.

66 *The Gonne-Yeats Letters 1893–1938*, p. 348.

67 Ibid., p. 348.

68 John Quinn to Maud Gonne (14 Mar. 1917), in *Too Long a Sacrifice*, p. 189.

69 John Quinn to Maud Gonne (13 Mar. 1911 and 30 May 1911), in ibid., p. 71, 75.

70 Maud Gonne, 'The real criminals', in *Irish Worker* (1 Nov. 1913), in Steele, *Maud Gonne's Irish Nationalist Writings*, p. 156.

71 *The Gonne-Yeats Letters 1893–1938*, p. 347.

72 Letter from Maud Gonne to John Quinn (15 July 1915), in *Too Long a Sacrifice*, p. 155.

73 Letter from Maud Gonne to John Quinn (17 Oct. 1915), in ibid., p. 160.

74 *The Gonne-Yeats Letters 1893–1938*, pp 347–8.

75 Ibid., p. 363.

Chapter 7

1 See Janis and Richard Londraville (eds), *Too Long a Sacrifice: The Letters of Maud Gonne and John Quinn* (Selinsgrove, 1999), p. 166.

2 Seán T. O'Kelly, Witness statement for the Bureau of Military History (hereafter, BMH WS), available at http://www.bureauofmilitaryhistory.ie/reels/bmh/BMH.WS1765%20PART%202.pdf.

3 Seán Enright, *Easter Rising 1916: The Trials* (Kildare, 2014), p. 147.

4 Dillon, Geraldine, notes, 3 July 1973. Research Files of Conrad Balliet. Series 2 Interviews, 1937, 1973–8 Box 1 Folders 18–41, AV1.

5 Letter from W. B. Yeats to Lady Gregory (18 Sept. 1917), in Allan Wade (ed.), *The Letters of W. B. Yeats* (London, 1955), p. 632.

6 Anna MacBride White and A. Norman Jeffares (eds), *The Gonne-Yeats Letters 1893–1938: Always Your Friend* (London, 1992), p. 391.

7 Yeats is quoted by Ezra Pound in a letter (28 Dec. 1918), in *The Selected Letters of Ezra Pound to John Quinn: 1915–1924* (Durham, 1991), p. 170.

8 Letter from Maud Gonne to John Quinn (16 Aug. 1916), in *Too Long a Sacrifice*, p. 176.

9 Letter from Maud Gonne to John Quinn (30 Apr. 1916), in ibid., p. 168.

10 Letter from John Quinn to Maud Gonne (29 July 1916), in ibid., p. 170.

11 'Resignation of Mr Birrell', House of Commons debate (03 May 1916) vol 82 cc30–9.

12 Letter from Maud Gonne to John Quinn (11 May 1916), in *Too Long a Sacrifice*, p. 169.

13 Letter from John Quinn to Maud Gonne (28 May 1916), in ibid., p. 200.

14 Letter from Father Augustine to Maud Gonne (22 June 1917), in ibid., p. 201.

15 Letter from John Quinn to Maud Gonne (29 July 1916), in ibid., p. 172.

16 Letter from Maud Gonne to John Quinn (11 May 1916), in ibid., p. 169.

17 Gonne did, however, use her marital status to secure a military pension in 1933.

18 Letter from Maud Gonne to John Quinn (16 Aug. 1916), in *Too Long a Sacrifice*, pp 176–7.

19 Letter from Maud Gonne to John Quinn (11 May 1916), in ibid., p. 169. Gonne writes 'The French people are thoroughly horrified at the English method of reprisal, but because of their alliance their press is silent & no word is said of Ireland —.'

20 Letter from Maud Gonne to John Quinn (16 Aug. 1916), in *Too Long a Sacrifice*, p. 177.

21 Letter from Maud Gonne to John Quinn (16 Aug. 1916), in ibid., p. 177.

22 Letter from John Quinn to Maud Gonne (17 July 1917), in ibid., p. 204. Quinn writes: 'Personally, I am more interested in winning the war than I am in settling the Irish question. Of course, I am interested in both. But if the Germans win there will be no English or Irish question to settle or talk about.' Quinn also privately disagreed with Gonne's propaganda campaign in America, writing to Frank Hugh O'Donnell on 12 Apr. 1914: 'The "millions of Irish Americans" that you allude to are a fiction. They don't know conditions on the other side; they largely think in packs; their thought about Ireland is the traditional one starting from Parnell's days down, and it is hopeless to attempt to change them.' See *Too Long a Sacrifice*, p. 254.

23 W. B. Yeats, 'Easter, 1916', in Daniel Albright (ed.), *W. B. Yeats: The Poems* (London 1992), p. 229.

24 *The Gonne-Yeats Letters 1893–1938*, p. 384.

25 Ibid.

26 PRO 903 8, cited by Conrad Balliet, 'For the love of Maud', p. 145. Series 3 Research files of Conrad Balliet Box 2–Box 5: Folder 5; OP1; Ethel Mannin records that Gonne thought 'Easter 1916' 'inadequate for the occasion'. See Conrad Balliet interview notes, conducted 24 June 1973.

27 James Stephens, 'The Spring in Ireland, 1916', in *Green Branches* (Macmillan, 1916), np.

28 Letter from Ezra Pound to John Quinn (20 Nov. 1918).

29 Ethel Mannin, Conrad Balliet interview notes, conducted 24 June 1973, p. 2. Series 2 Interviews, 1937, 1973–8 Box 1. Folders 18–41, AV1.

30 'Letter from Director of British Control, Paris to Maud Gonne (2 July 1917), in *Too Long a Sacrifice*, p. 210.

31 See Gonne's BMH WS.

32 Ibid.

33 Letter from Home Office citing minute (11 Jan. 1918). Dublin Castle Records 1798–1926. Irish Government. Sinn Féin and Republican Suspects, 1899–1921 (CO 904, Boxes 193–216). Public Records Office, London, England. CO 904/208/258–260 Gale Document Number: GALE | SC5101862289.

34 Letter from Dublin Metropolitan Police (17 June 1918). Dublin Castle Records 1798–1926. Irish Government. Sinn Féin and Republican Suspects, 1899–1921 (CO 904, Boxes 193–216). Public Records Office, London, England. CO 904/208/258–260 Gale Document Number: GALE | SC5101862289.

35 Letter to Chief Commissioner (30 Nov. 1918). Dublin Castle Records 1798–1926. Irish Government. Sinn Féin and Republican Suspects, 1899–1921 (CO 904, Boxes 193–216). Public Records Office, London, England. CO 904/208/258–260 Gale Document Number: GALE | SC5101862289.

36 Letter from Ezra Pound to John Quinn (29 Jan. 1918), in D. D. Paige (ed.), *Selected Letters of Ezra Pound 1907–1941* (London, 1950), p. 131.

37 An appeal was submitted for their release on the grounds that the Order signed by the Chief Secretary of Ireland sentence them to internment in Frongoch rather than Holloway. See 'Irish prisoners', House of Commons debate (4 June 1918) vol 106 cc1406–7.

38 Ibid. (8 July 1918) vol 108 c34.

39 M. J. Kelly, *The Fenian Ideal and Irish Nationalism 1882–1916* (Rochester, 2009), p. 85.

40 Constance Markievicz, *The Prison Letters of Countess Markievicz* (London, 1986), pp 179–80.

41 Interview with Kit MacBride, 9 July 1974. Research Files of Conrad Balliet. Series 2 Interviews, 1937, 1973–8. Box 1: Folders 18–41, AV1, p. 1.

42 Dublin Castle Records. Irish Government. Sinn Féin and republican suspects, 1899–1921 (CO 904, Boxes 193–216). Public Records Office, London, England. CO 904/208/258–260. Gale Document Number: GALE | SC5101862289.

43 Letter from Ezra Pound to John Quinn (15 Nov. 1918), in Paige, *Selected Letters of Ezra Pound 1907–1941*, p. 140.

44 30 Nov. 1918. Dublin Castle Records. Irish Government. Sinn Féin and republican suspects, 1899–1921 (CO 904, Boxes 193–216). Public Records Office, London, England. CO 904/208/258–260. Gale Document Number: GALE | SC5101862289.

45 Letter from Maud Gonne to Max Wright, in *Daily Express*, about the conditions in Mountjoy Prison and the ill treatment of prisoners there by the Free State troops, undated [*c.* 1922–3].

46 Letter from Maud Gonne to Max Wright, *Daily Express*, [undated *c.* 1922–3].

47 Gonne, 'My experiences in prison', in *Irish Citizen* (June–July 1919), reprinted in Karen Steele (ed.), *Maud Gonne's Irish Nationalist Writings* (Dublin, 2004), pp 11–15.

Chapter 8

1 *Official Correspondence Relating to the Peace Negotiations June–September 1921* (Dublin, 1921).

2 Eileen O'Brien interview transcript, 11 July 1973. Research Files of Conrad Balliet. Series 2 Interviews, 1937, 1973–8 Box 1: Folders 18–41, AV1.

3 Ibid.

4 Maude Gonne, 'Condemnation of the Provisional Government', in Karen Steele (ed.), *Maud Gonne's Irish Nationalist Writings* (Dublin, 2004), p. 222.

5 Maud Gonne, *The Autobiography of Maud Gonne: A Servant of the Queen* (Chicago: 1995), p. 313.

6 See Gonne's witness statement from the Bureau of Military History (hereafter BMH WS).

7 Women's Prisoners' Defence League, 'To Irishmen and women' [n.d. c.1923] Department of Ephemera, National Library of Ireland (hereafter, NLI), EPH D130.

8 Seán McConville, *Irish Political Prisoners, 1848–1922: Theatres of War* (London, 2003), p. 634.

9 Letter from Maud Gonne to Max Wright, [undated, *c.* 1922–23], NLI Manuscripts (hereafter, MS) 15,001.

10 Gonne, 'Political prisoners: Outside and in', in *Voice of Ireland*, 1924, reprinted in Karen Steele (ed.), *Maud Gonne's Irish Nationalist Writings* (Dublin, 2004), p. 21.

11 Fragments of notes by Maud Gonne relating to an escape plan [for six Sinn Féin prisoners from Strangeway Gaol] [1919], NLI MS 11,409/3/19.

12 Francis Stuart interview transcript, 4 July 1973. Series 2 Interviews, 1937, 1973–8 Box 1: Folders 18–41, AV1.

13 Ibid. According to Stuart Gonne was never a member of the IRA, which had no opening for women.

14 Margaret Ward, *Maud Gonne: A Life* (London, 1993), pp 123–4.

15 Ibid., p. 124.

16 Francis Stuart interview transcript, July 4, 1973.

17 On 20 Mar. 1920 the Lord Lieutenant referred to two revolvers seized from a van containing furniture belonging to Maud Gonne. Dublin Castle Records 1798–1926. Irish Government. Sinn Féin and republican suspects, 1899–1921 (CO 904, Boxes 193–216). Public Records Office, London, England. CO 904/208/258–260 Gale Document Number: GALE | SC5101862289; See Gonne BMH WS for her account of the raid.

18 Steele, (ed.), *Maud Gonne's Irish Nationalist Writings 1895–1946*, p. 188.

19 Transcript of Katherine Somers, Tony and May Woods and Mercedes Keating Interviews. Research Files of Conrad Balliet. Series 2 Interviews, 1937, 1973–8 Box 1: Folders 18–41, AV1.

20 Interview with Sheila Humphreys O'Donoghue, quoted by Ward in *Maud Gonne: A Life*, p. 136.

21 For example see photograph 0504/031 captioned 'Women protest outside Mountjoy Jail (*c.* 1922)', in the RTÉ Cashman Collection (online).

22 Richard Bennett, *The Black and Tans* (London, 1959), p. 100.

23 Ian Kenneally, *The Paper Wall: Newspapers and Propaganda in Ireland 1919–1921* (Cork, 2008), p. 69.

24 W. B. Yeats, 'Ireland, 1921–1931', in Colton Johnson (ed.), *The Collected Works of W. B. Yeats, Vol. X, Later Articles and Reviews* (New York, 2000), p. 231.

25 PRO 903 8, cited by Conrad Balliet, 'For the love of Maud', p. 144. Series 3 Research files of Conrad Balliet Box 2–Box 5: Folder 5; OP1. This was the view of Ethel Mannin in an interview with Balliet. See Eileen O'Brien, interview transcript, 11 July 1973.

26 Transcript of Michael MacLiammoir Interview. Research Files of Conrad Balliet. Series 1 Correspondence, *c.* 1902–50 Box 1: Folders 1–17.

27 Transcript of Katherine Somers, Tony and May Woods and Mercedes Keating Interviews.

28 Ibid.

29 Interview with Kit MacBride, 9 July 1974, p. 1. Research Files of Conrad Balliet. Series 2 Interviews, 1937, 1973–8. Box 1: Folders 18–41, AV1, p. 4.

30 Francis Stuart interview transcript, July 4, 1973, [includes Conrad Balliet's notes regarding the Stuart interview and his interview of Monk Gibbon].

31 Ibid.

32 Ibid.

33 Máire Comerford papers, University College Dublin Archives (hereafter, UCDA), LA18/8(3).

34 Margaret Ward, *Hanna Sheehy Skeffington: Suffragette and Sinn Féiner: Her Memoirs and Political Writings* (Dublin, 2017), p. 175; Francis Stuart mentions that the White Cross work was supported by American money for aid for prisoners and families of prisoners. See Francis Stuart interview, conducted 4 July 1973.

35 Máire Comerford papers, UCDA, LA18/8(5).

36 Ibid.

37 Ibid., LA18/8(7).

38 Ibid.

39 Ultach, *Orange Terror: The Partition of Ireland. A Reprint from the Capuchin Annual*, 1943, p. 30, Public Record Office of Northern Ireland (hereafter, PRONI) D3257/1.

40 Maud Gonne, 'Condemnation of the Provisional Government', in *Éire* (22 Sept. 1923) in Steele, *Maud Gonne's Irish Nationalist Writings*, p. 221.

41 Ibid.

42 Maud Gonne MacBride, 'An appeal to our race', [n.p.] PRONI D2991/B/59/5.

43 Maud Gonne MacBride, 'Comments', in Ultach, *The Orange Terror*, p. 30.

44 Ibid.

45 'Madame Gonne MacBride and Orangeism', in *Londonderry Sentinel* (11 Apr. 1939), p. 5.

46 In defiance of the Coercion Act the masthead of *Prison Bars* read: 'We stand for the freedom of the press', in 'To readers of *Prison Bars*', Gonne thanked readers for their support of the newssheet, noting: 'If they did not get their money's worth in printed matter they helped *Prison Bars* to prove by its existence that it is always possible to defeat a Coercion Act no matter how drastic, and if like occasion arose we are prepared to restart this paper on the same basis.' NLI MS 49,360.

47 Letter from Maud Gonne to Joseph McGarrity 3 Oct. [1937] NLI MS 17,456/8.

48 *Prison Bars*, No.18. Oct. 1838 PRONI D2991/E/12/1.

49 'Madame Gonne MacBride and Orangeism', p. 5.

50 Letter from Maud Gonne to Joseph McGarrity 3rd Oct. [1937] NLI MS 17,456/8; *Prison Bars*, No. 18. Oct. 1838 PRONI D2991/E/12/1.

51 'Madame Gonne MacBride and Orangeism', p. 5.

52 Ibid.

53 'The Irish Constitution', in *Prison Bars* (3 July 1937), reprinted in Ward, *Hanna Sheehy Skeffington*, p. 342.

54 Maud Gonne MacBride, 'Comments', in Ultach, *The Orange Terror*, pp 30–1.

55 RTE transcription: Series of talks by Maud Gonne, May 1937 [MSS771], Series 2 Interviews, 1937, 1973–8 Box 1: Folders 18–41, AV1, p. 22.

56 Transcript of untitled radio broadcast by Maud Gonne, May 1937, Series 2 Interviews, 1937, 1973–8 Box 1: Folders 18–41, AV1, p. 2.

57 Ibid., p. 27.

Chapter 9

1 Maud Gonne, 'Yeats and Ireland', *Scattering Branches* (London, 1940), p. 25.

2 Francis Stuart interview transcript, 4 July 1973; Gonne, 'A protest addressed to AE: To the editor of the *Irish Statesman*', in *Éire* (20 Sept. 1924), Karen Steele (ed.), *Maud Gonne's Irish Nationalist Writings* (Dublin, 2004), p. 225.

3 Francis Stuart interview transcript, 4 July 1973.

4 Ibid.

5 Ibid.

6 Maud Gonne MacBride interview, no date, with notes by Conrad Balliet and photocopy of published interview. Series 2 Interviews, 1937, 1973–8 Box 1: Folders 18–41, AV1.

7 Francis Stuart interview transcript, 4 July 1973.

8 Gonne, 'Yeats and Ireland', p. 27.

9 Anna MacBride White and A. Norman Jeffares (eds), *The Gonne-Yeats Letters 1893–1938: Always Your Friend* (London, 1992), p. 357.

10 'Maud Gonne MacBride', in *The Derry Journal* (1 May 1953), p. 2.

11 Maud Gonne, *The Autobiography of Maud Gonne: A Servant of the Queen* (Chicago, 1995), p. 178.

12 Francis Stuart interview transcript, 4 July 1973.

13 W. B. Yeats, *The Trembling of the Veil* (London, 1922), p. 235.

14 Gonne, 'I saw the Queen', in *A Servant of the Queen*, n.p.

15 Frank Gallagher, *Days of Fear* (London, 1929), p. 56.

Select Bibliographical Details

Balfour, Arthur (1848–1930) was a member of the Conservative Party who served as Prime Minister of the United Kingdom from 1902 to 1905. During the Plan of Campaign he suppressed agrarian rest in his role as Chief Secretary for Ireland.

Comerford, Máire (1892–1982) was a teacher and republican activist and journalist. She was inspired to join the nationalist movement after attending a performance at the Abbey Theatre. After witnessing the 1916 Rising, Comerford joined her local branch of Sinn Féin in Gorey, Wicklow. She joined Cumann na mBan and the White Cross and took an active role on the republican side during the War of Independence. When she was imprisoned by Free State authorities in Mountjoy Prison, Comerford went on hunger strike. Despite feeling that the Irish cause was betrayed by the Treaty, she worked as a journalist for de Valera's newspaper, the *Irish Press*. Inspired by Gonne, Comerford travelled to America in 1924 on behalf of Sinn Féin to raise funds for the republican causes and devoted much of her energy into campaigning for better conditions for political prisoners.

Cosgrave, William T. (1880–1965) was the leader of Fine Gael from 1934–44. He was the first elected head of government in the Irish Free State, holding the role of President of Dáil Éireann from September 1922 to December 1922.

Davitt, Michael (1846–1906) was an Irish nationalist and founder of the Irish Land League. At the age of four Davitt was forced to leave his home in Straide, Co. Mayo when his family were evicted due to being in arrears of rent. The family emigrated to Lancashire and Davitt began work in a mill at the age of ten. In May 1857 Davitt lost his right arm as a result of an accident while operating the mill's machinery. In 1865 Davitt joined the Fenian movement. He joined the IRB in 1865, becoming its secretary in 1868. In 1870 Davitt was arrested for sending firearms to Ireland and was sentenced to 15 years in prison but was released in 1877. He publicised his experiences as an evicted tenant in America in lecture tours in 1878 and 1882. His increasing association with the Irish Parliamentary Party led to his expulsion from the supreme council of the IRB in 1880. He welcomed Gladstone's second Home Rule bill (1893) as a 'pact of peace'.

Despard, Charlotte (1844–1939) was a socialist, nationalist, suffragist and writer. She married into a wealthy Irish Protestant family from Laois. After her husband's death in 1870 she moved to London where she provided aid to the poorest residents of Battersea. She joined the Social Democratic Federation and the Independent Labour Party. Her conversion to Catholicism in 1898 was coupled with an increasing interest in Ireland. She became involved in the socialist movement, speaking at rallies during the 1913 Lockout. In 1921, she purchased Roebuck House and began to work closely with Maud Gonne. Together they publicised Black and Tan atrocities, provided employment to republican ex-prisoners and supported Catholic exiles from the North.

Devoy, John (1842–1928) became Chief Organizer of Fenians in the British Army. In 1867, he was sentenced to 15 years of hard labour for planning an uprising with the IRB. Upon his early release from prison in 1871, Devoy moved to New York, where he worked as a journalist, organised the American Land League and became leader of Clan na Gael. He organised a lecture tour in America for Michal Davitt and a visit by Roger Casement, with whom he raised money for arms for the 1916 Rising. He was an important American contact for Maud Gonne and John MacBride on their 1901 lecture tour.

Egan, James (*c.* 1844–1909) was born in Limerick but relocated to Birmingham to work. He became acquainted with John Daly, with whom he was charged and sentenced to 20 years imprisonment for high treason when explosives were allegedly found in Egan's garden, although a case was raised that they had been planted by the police. He became close friends with Tom Clarke in prison and on his release he began to work for the Amnesty Association. He also went to the United States to campaign for the release of Fenian prisoners.

FitzGerald, Thomas Joseph (1888–1947), known as Desmond FitzGerald, was a poet, MP (1918–22) and TD (1918–43). Raised in London by Irish parents, he became a member of an imagist group of London poets. He adopted the name Desmond to associate himself with his Irish ancestry and he learnt the Irish language while living in London. Following a short time living in France after his marriage, he moved to Ireland in 1913. He joined the Irish Volunteers in 1914 and organised a Volunteers group in County Kerry. In 1915 FitzGerald was imprisoned for making a speech against recruitment during the First World War. He launched the underground *Irish Bulletin* in November 1919 and used his London connections to make contact with foreign journalists. As Director of Publicity (1919–21), Minister for Publicity (1921–2) and Minister for External Affairs (1922–7), he played key administrative roles at the time of the foundation of the Irish State. He oversaw Ireland's successful application to join the League of Nations in 1923.

Griffith, Arthur (1871–1922) began his career as an apprentice printer and compositor. He joined the IRB and fought for the Boers in South Africa in 1896. When he established the United Irishman with William Rooney on his return to Ireland in 1898, Maud Gonne funded the venture. Griffith founded Sinn Féin and headed the Irish delegation in the negotiations of 1921 which led to the establishment of the Irish Free State, of which he was the first President.

Harrington, Timothy (1851–1910), known as Tim Harrington, was a journalist, barrister, and MP. Harrington was secretary and chief organiser of the Irish National League and he devised the Plan of Campaign in 1886 with William O'Brien. Harrington edited two newspapers, *United Ireland* and the *Kerry Sentinel*. He was Lord Mayor of Dublin from 1901–04, during which time he came under fire from nationalists for supporting King Edward VII's visit to Dublin. Harrington persuaded Gonne to make a political speech at the Barrow-in-Furness by-election, which secured the victory of Irish candidate, James Duncan.

Hyde, Douglas (1860–1949) was a Gaelic scholar, founder of the Gaelic League and first President of Ireland. Joining the Society for Preservation of the Language in 1877 and the Gaelic Union in 1878, Hyde began a lifelong campaign to restore Irish as the national language. From 1879 he began publishing original Irish-language poems and literary articles. He met Gonne through his affiliation with the Contemporary Club. Between 1901 and 1905 he was a prominent figure in Irish Literary Theatre, collaborating with Lady Gregory in writing plays in Irish. In 1905–6 he undertook an American fund-raising tour organised by John Quinn. In 1909 Hyde became the first Professor of Irish at UCD.

MacBride, John (1865–1916), was an officer in the Boer army and an Irish republican. Born in Mayo, MacBride emigrated to the Transvaal Republic in 1895, initially working in a goldmine outside Johannesburg. When war broke out in October 1899 McBride established and led the Irish Transvaal brigade to fight on the Boer side against the British. After the war MacBride moved to France where, through fellow soldier Willie Rooney, he met Maud Gonne. After unsuccessfully standing as an independent nationalist in the South Mayo by-election of February 1900, MacBride agreed to join Gonne on a lecture tour of America. MacBride and Gonne married in 1903 and had a son, Seán, in 1904. The marriage foundered, allegedly due to MacBride's drinking and they separated in 1905 with Gonne retaining custody of Seán. MacBride was unaware of plans for insurrection in Easter 1916. Stumbling on it by accident, he was recruited by Thomas MacDonagh and he became second-in-command of Jacob's factory. He was court martialled and executed for his role in the Rising in May 1916.

Markievicz, Constance (née Gore-Booth) (1868–1927), republican and labour activist, was born into a wealthy London family that relocated to Lissadell, an estate in Sligo owned by the Gore-Booth family. In 1893, Constance moved to London to study art. Studying art in Paris in 1898, she met Count Casimir Dunin-Markievicz, a Polish artist. They married in 1900 and had a daughter in 1901. After separating from her husband, Markievicz joined Inghinidhe na hÉireann and established Fianna Éireann. She played a key role in the 1913 Lockout, organising soup kitchens in Dublin for striking workers and their families. Markievicz became honorary treasurer of the Irish Citizen Army. She was sentenced to death on account of her role as second-in-command of an Irish Citizen Army unit in St Stephen's Green during the Rising, but her sentence was commuted to imprisonment. While incarcerated, she successfully stood as a Sinn Féin candidate in a Dublin election, but refused to take her seat at Westminster. She was released in June 1917. When she returned to Ireland in March 1919, she became Minister for Labour in the first Dáil Éireann.

Millevoye, Lucien (1815–1918) was a far-right French politician, writer and editor. He was an ardent supporter of General Georges Boulanger, Minister of War in France, who was focused on restoring the lost eastern territories of Alsace and Lorraine to France. After Boulanger's suicide in 1891, Millevoye focused on editing the evening newspaper, *La Patrie*, and he later became chairman of the French army's committee on aviation.

Milligan, Alice (1865–1953) was a poet of the Irish Literary Revival. She founded two nationalist publications *The Northern Patriot* and later *The Shan Van Vocht*, a monthly literary magazine published in Belfast from 1896 to 1899. She also founded branches of the Irish Women's Association and became its president.

Molony, Helena (1884–1967) joined Inghinidhe na hÉireann after hearing a speech by Maud Gonne in 1903, and in 1907 she became the society's secretary. Gonne and Moloney founded a women's nationalist periodical *Bean na nÉireann* with Molony becoming its editor from 1908–11. She acted with Inghinidhe na hÉireann and later the Irish Citizen Army (women's group). Molony assisted Constance Markievicz in the founding of the republican scouts' organisation, Na Fianna Éireann, and worked as secretary for the Irish Citizen Army. After taking part in an attack on Dublin Castle during the Easter Rising, Molony was arrested and interned in England. After her release in December 1916, she became active in the Irish Trade Union Congress, ultimately becoming its president.

Mulcahy, Richard James (1886–1971) was an army general and commander-in-chief for the Irish Republican Army (IRA), who fought in the 1916 Easter Rising and served as Chief-of-Staff in the IRA during the War of Independence. He became a commander of the pro-Treaty side in the Irish Civil War and became known for the ruthless suppression of republican opposition. With the Women's Prisoners' Defence League Maud Gonne organised a protest outside Mulcahy's house against the murder of prisoners of war.

O'Brien, Patrick (*c*.1847–1917), known as Pat O'Brien, came to Parnell's attention through his work for the Land League and, at Parnell's request, stood successfully in a by-election and became a member of the Irish Parliamentary Party representing North Monaghan. O'Brien became very active in the Plan of Campaign in 1887 to 1890, working with Maud Gonne to help evicted tenants in Donegal. She regularly used photographs taken by O'Brien on her lecture tours.

O'Higgins, Kevin (1892–1927) was a member of Sinn Féin and Cumann na nGaedheal who took the pro-Treaty side in the Irish Free State, becoming a TD in 1922. He signed the execution orders of 77 political prisoners and was assassinated by the IRA in Dublin in 1927.

O'Leary, John (1830–1907) was a journalist and editor of the *Irish People*, which was suppressed in 1865 when O'Leary was sentenced to 20 years penal servitude for treason-felony on account of the publication. O'Leary was released in 1871 on the grounds that he did not return to Ireland. He lived in Paris until 1885. He visited America to secure funds for the Irish Republican Brotherhood (IRB) with which he was closely linked. O'Leary was an important nationalist networker in the 1880s and 1890s, founding the Contemporary Club and contributing to the formation of the Young Ireland League and the Pan-Celtic Literary Group, and he provided financial support to the Gaelic Athletic Association. Although a committed nationalist, O'Leary's loyalties were divided in relation to land ownership and eviction; he opposed the Plan of Campaign, which was antipathetic to his own financial interests as a landowner.

Parnell, Charles Stewart (1846–91) was an Anglo-Irish landowner turned nationalist politician. After being educated in England Parnell returned to his home in Avondale, Wicklow. In 1874 he became High Sheriff of Wicklow. In 1874 he ran unsuccessfully for parliament for Dublin and then in April 1875 he won Meath in a by-election. He embarked on a policy of obstructionism in his parliamentary career. Parnell is also credited with what was termed the 'New Departure' in Irish politics, successfully uniting Fenians, the parliamentary movement and the land movement. He toured America where he was so well received that he was dubbed 'the uncrowned king of Ireland'. Parnell became leader of the Irish Parliamentary Party, which he founded, in 1882. In 1890 the party split following revelations of Parnell's extra-marital affair with Katharine O'Shea. Parnell died in October 1891.

Quinn, John (1870–1924) was a lawyer and art collector. He met W. B. Yeats in 1902 and helped to found the Abbey Theatre in the same year and arranged Yeats's tour of American from 1903 to 1904. Quinn successfully defended Lady Gregory and her actors when an injunction was passed on *The Playboy of the Western World* in Philadelphia on the grounds of indecency. He also financially supported James Joyce and defended him when legal action was taken against the *Little Review* in 1920 in which Ulysses was serialised in. Quinn successfully defended the novel which he claimed could not corrupt as it was incomprehensible.

Ryan, Mark (1844–1940) was recruited to the IRB by Michael Davitt in 1865 after his family were evicted from their home in Galway. He relocated to England, settling in London, where he became a prominent member of the IRB, ultimately becoming a member of the Supreme Council. In 1867 he returned to Galway to take part in a Fenian rebellion, which failed on account of poor organisation. In 1892 he founded the Amnesty Associations.

Stead, William T. (1849–1912) was a journalist and editor best known as a pioneer of investigative journalism. He drew attention to a number of social and political issues, opposing the poor law and campaigning for compulsory primary and secondary education, universal suffrage and collective bargaining in industrial relations. He supported Home Rule for Ireland. He is best remembered for his controversial 'Maiden Tribute of Modern Babylon' articles, written to support a bill to raise the age of consent from 13 to 16, and also for his untimely death as a passenger on the Titanic in April 1912.

Stephens, James (1825–1901) was a Dublin-born poet and novelist of the Irish literary revival who also wrote for the *Irish Citizen* and the *Irish Worker*. Abandoned by his widowed mother, Stephens was raised in an orphanage. An education in a charity school enabled him to secure work as a typist in a solicitor's firm. He became involved with the Revival movement after the publication of his first volume of poetry in 1908. Stephens was a co-founder of the *Irish Review*, a nationalist forum for discussion of Irish arts. The journalism he wrote in the wake of the Rising was published as a volume entitled *The Insurrection in Dublin* (1916), and he also published a collection of poems entitled *Green Branches* (1916).

Stopford Green, Alice (1847–1929), was an Irish nationalist and historian. She moved to England where she met and married historian John Richard Green. After his death in 1883 she moved from England, where she had lived during her marriage, back to Ireland, and she established herself as a writer, also known as Mrs J. R. Green. She wrote *The Making of Ireland and its Undoing* (1908) and she also published on female suffrage, which she supported, considering women to be inherently disadvantaged in the male-dominated world of politics. However, she was elected to Seanad Éireann in 1922 and served as an independent senator until her death in 1929.

Taylor, John Francis (1853–1902) was a barrister, journalist and man of letters. He became a leader-writer on the *Freeman's Journal* in the 1880s. He was also deeply involved with the Contemporary Club, where he met Maud Gonne. At Gonne's request, he successfully defended an American IRB man who worked under the name 'Ivory'. He later successfully defended Gonne in her libel suit against the editor of the *Figaro*, Ramsey Colles.

Teeling, Charles was a vice-president of the Young Ireland Society who was ultimately expelled by a committee of the Society. A series of letters between W. B. Yeats and John O'Leary comment on Teeling acting as a spy who publicly slandered Maud Gonne.

Yeats, William Butler (1865–1939) was an Irish poet born in Dublin who became a central figure of the Irish Literary Revival. His first volume of poetry *The Wanderings of Oisin and Other Poems*, which drew on Irish legend and set out to establish a distinctive Irish literature, gained critical acclaim upon its publication in 1889. Yeats established himself in London where he became a member of the Rhymers' Club, which brought him into contact with notable Irish literary figures in *fin de siècle* London, including Oscar Wilde and George Bernard Shaw. He spent his life primarily in London and in Sligo at the estate of fellow-writer Augusta Gregory. In 1889 he met and fell in love with Maud Gonne who inspired many of his poems for the rest of his life. Yeats contributed to Gonne's propaganda campaign in the nationalist press. Yeats and Gregory collaborated with Edward Martyn an artistic patron and playwright to establish the Irish Literary Theatre, which produced nationalist plays in Dublin from May 1889. The most famous play of the Revival was Yeats's *Cathleen ní Houlihan* (1902), in which Gonne was cast in the leading role. He subsequently helped to found the Abbey Theatre in Dublin. Gonne refused Yeats's numerous proposals of marriage and in October 1917 he married Bertha Georgie Hyde Lees, known as George. Yeats memorialised Gonne's husband, John MacBride as a 'drunken, vainglorious lout' in 'Easter 1916' and gradually political differences increasingly separated Yeats and Gonne. In December 1922, Yeats was elected Senator of the Irish Free State. In 1923, he was awarded the Nobel Prize in Literature.

Index

1913 Lockout 68–9
1916 Rising 4–5, 54–6, 58, 71–5

Allgood, Sara 52–3
Anglo-Irish Treaty 39, 78–81, 84

Balfour, Arthur 25
Bean na hÉireann 3, 63, 69
British War Office 5

Cathleen ni Houlihan 5, 16, 30, 32, 52–8, 90
Cavanagh MacDowell, Maeve 55
Childers, Erskine 81
Coercion Act of 1923 80, 86
Comerford, Máire 44, 53–4, 83–4
Connolly, James 29, 33, 41, 59
Cosgrave, William T. 31, 80

de Valera, Éamon 54, 79, 86–8
Defence of the Realm Act 76
Derry Journal 89
Despard, Charlotte 80–4, 88
Devoy, John 36, 39
Dillon, Geraldine 71
Duncan, James 19

Egan, James 36

First World War 17
Fitzgerald, Desmond 82, 85
Freeman's Journal 30

German Empire 76
'The German Plot' 76
Gonne, Edith 7–8
Gonne, Edith Maud
    acting 5, 11, 16, 19, 52–8, 90 *see also* Cathleen ni Houlihan
activism
    anti-Jubilee demonstration 6, 17, 33–5
    Barrow-in-Furness campaign 19, 25, 37
    'Battle of Coulson Avenue' 62–3
    'Battle of the Rotunda' 34
    eviction rights 10, 15, 18–19, 25, 29, 34, 41, 52, 55–7, 59
    prisoner defence 3, 17, 19, 24, 30–1, 36, 67, 76, 78, 80–1, 84, 86–9 *see also Prison Bars* and Women's Prisoners' Defence League
belief in reincarnation 22
birth and early life 7–13
as Chair of the National Aid Association 84

and the Civil War 79, 81–4
conversion to Catholicism 60–1
death 89
divorce 64–7
education 7–9
imprisonment 77–8
and the IRB 49
lecture tours 3, 11, 19–20, 25–6, 29,
     36–41, 47, 50–1
legacy 89–91
painting
     Celtic Wonder Tales 68
as propagandist 2, 16–18, 25–6,
     33, 35–6, 40, 49–52, 58, 60, 62–6,
     82–3, 86
relationship with MacBride 6,
     49–51, 59–61, 63–8, 73–5
relationship with Millevoye 2,
     4–5, 12–13, 18–20, 28, 32,
     48–9, 77
relationship with Yeats 4, 21–2,
     40, 48, 52–3, 57–8, 60, 65–6, 70–2,
     75, 82, 89–90
thoughts on the 1937 Irish
     Constitution 87
writings
     A Servant of the Queen 1, 4, 5,
          7–10, 12, 15, 18–19, 48, 60,
          63, 90
     articles
          'An Appeal to our Race' 85
          'Atrocités dans les Bagnes
               Anglais' 6
          'Branding' 31
          'Le Martyre de l'Irlande' 26,
               28
          'Reine de la Disette' ('The
               Famine Queen') 26, 29, 45

'The Irish Press' 63
'The Right to Life and the
     Rights of Property' 59
'Those Who Are Suffering
     for Ireland' 31
'To Irishmen and Women'
     80
'The Voice of the Poor' 27
'Un Peuple Opprimé' ('An
     Oppressed People') 28
plays
     Dawn 55–9
     'Poems of a Dragoon' 47
Gonne, Georges 12, 20–2, 40
death 21–2
Gonne, Iseult 12, 18, 67–8, 76, 81
Gonne, Kathleen 7, 9–10, 64, 77
Gonne, Margaretta Rose 7
Gonne, Tommy 7–10
Gore-Booth, Eva 76
Grennan, Julia 55
Griffith, Arthur 3, 20, 33, 40, 45, 49–52,
     79–80, 82, 84–5

Harrington, Timothy 12, 19, 34
Hermetic Order of the Golden
     Dawn 22
Hyde, Douglas 15

Inghinidhe na hÉireann 41–4, 47,
     51–2, 54, 61–3, 68–9, 87, 89, 91
Irish Literary Theatre 52
Irish Republican Prisoners'
     Dependents' Fund 84

Journal des Voyage 28, 34

King Edward VII 34, 62

L'Irlande Libre 28–9, 33, 39–40
La Revue International 28
Lady Gregory 21, 52–3, 58–9

MacBride, John 4–6, 49–51, 56, 59–61, 63–7, 71, 73–5
  death 71
MacBride, Kit 9, 83
MacBride, Seán 9, 18, 66–7, 79, 81
Markievicz, Constance 4, 47, 72, 76–7
Millevoye, Lucien 2, 4–5, 12–13, 18–21, 28, 32, 41, 48–9, 60, 77
Milligan, Alice 41, 51
Molony, Helena 4, 54, 63
'The Mothers' 81
Mulcahy, Richard 31, 80

National Library 15, 33
Nic Shiubhlaigh, Máire 52–3

O'Brien, Patrick 17–19, 23, 25, 32
O'Farrell, Elizabeth 4, 55
O'Higgins, Kevin 31
O'Leary, John 14–15, 17, 22, 33, 40–1
O'Neill, Maire 52–3
O'Rahilly, The 89

Parnell, Charles Stewart 5, 21, 29, 33, 37, 59
The Playboy of the Western World 58
Pound, Ezra 72, 77–8
Prison Bars 3, 86–7 *see also* Women's

Prisoners' Defence League and prisoner defence

Queen Victoria 1, 6, 32–4, 43
Quinn, John 58, 68–70, 72–5

Radio Éireann 87
Republic of Ireland Act (1948) 87
Rooney, Willie 3, 40, 80
Ryan, Mark 36, 49

Sexton, Thomas 25
Sheehy-Skeffington, Hanna 3, 84
Stead, William T. 5, 24, 26 29
Stephens, James 75
Stopford Green, Alice 53, 82
Stuart, Francis 78, 81, 83, 88

Taylor, John Francis 14, 17, 32, 38
Teeling, Charles 30

United Irishman 3, 6, 20, 22, 26–7, 33, 40–1, 43, 45, 50, 55, 58

Women's Peace Committee 79
Women's Prisoners' Defence League 3, 80, 84, 86–7

Yeats, William Butler 4, 15–16, 21, 26–9, 36, 40–1, 48, 51–5, 57–8, 60, 63–7, 70–2, 74–5, 78, 82, 89–90
Young Ireland League 22, 40